Impacting Generations: How  Nations is shocking in its ra...... prayer is not to be released o.......... ..., or the "prayer warriors" of the c....., ordinary people can release mountain-moving prayer. We can pray in the context of *Impacting Generations* and influencing the future of nations. The legacies of nation-shaping prayer by Intercessors for America (IFA) cofounders Derek Prince and John Beckett are growing brighter through the revelation released by IFA's current president, Dave Kubal. Thank you, Dave, for the new light. It couldn't be timelier.

—*Dutch Sheets*
Founder, Dutch Sheets Ministries and Give Him 15

David Kubal's *Impacting Generations: How Ordinary People Can Influence the Future of Nations* is a profoundly revelatory book that should be read almost as an addition to Derek Prince's internationally acclaimed *Shaping History through Prayer and Fasting*. Prince cofounded Intercessors for America, and now Kubal, Prince's successor as president of IFA, builds on that legacy. Drawing from the biblical understanding of the Abrahamic covenant, Kubal reveals how God's promise to bless all nations through God's chosen people is still active.

This book is an urgent, biblical call for intercessors, leaders, and believers everywhere to gain understanding, rise up, fast, and pray, confront diabolically inspired ideologies that destroy families and nations, possess the gates of enemies, and take their places on the stage of history. Thank you, David, for carrying on and fulfilling Derek Prince's dream of impacting generations through your revelation.

—*Lou Engle*
President, Lou Engle Ministries

Some fifty years ago, I had the privilege of helping found Intercessors for America. Years later, I headed the team that hired Dave Kubal as our CEO. We immediately knew we had found the right person, which has been affirmed repeatedly. His appointment to lead IFA came with an anointing. He is an excellent, effective, and inspired leader.

Reading *Impacting Generations* has lifted my admiration for Dave to a new level. Here, he articulates the unique role of the intercessor as clearly and powerfully as I have ever seen. Through prayer and intercession, we have an opportunity to shape America's future in profound and lasting ways. This book will spur a movement to guide our nation ever closer to God's majestic design.

—*John D. Beckett*
Cofounding member, Intercessors for America
Chairman, The Beckett Companies

Prayer is not intercession! This book will describe the biblical understanding of true intercession and how you can impact nations for future generations.

—*Pastor Paula White-Cain*
Founder and president, Paula White Ministries
Founder and president, National Faith Advisory Board
President, City of Destiny
Special government employee and senior advisor,
White House Faith Office

Dave Kubal's *Impacting Generations* masterfully explains the importance and differences between intercession and prayer. That issue alone is worth reading the entire book!

I appreciate Dave's direct and simple approach to many issues we are dealing with in the church today. The church has much to correct in our theology and how we are to pray and intercede. This book will dispel myths you probably thought were in Scripture and give you the path forward!

Let's all get back to Scripture and let God show us how to take our place and authority. Underline and highlight this book. It will be a valued go-to resource in your library. Get ready to impact generations!

—*Gene Bailey*
Host, *FlashPoint*

David Kubal knows how to weave the theological with the practical in *Impacting Generations*. His heart for all nations, especially America, comes clearly into focus, emphasizing the often-forgotten tools of prayer and intercession. He reminds us that God does extraordinary things through ordinary people.

—*Pastor Gary Hamrick*
Senior Pastor, Cornerstone Chapel, Leesburg, VA

Dave Kubal has written a history-making book. It is eye-opening and puts in perspective where we are as a nation and where we need to go. It will be a manual for generations to possess the gates of the enemy.

—*Cindy Jacobs*
Cofounder, Generals International

David Kubal is profoundly respected among faith leaders. It is wise to heed what he has to say. The lost covenant of Abraham is critical for the body of Christ to understand if we want to impact generations to come.

—*Jim Garlow, PhD*
Founder and CEO, Well Versed

Dave Kubal is leading monumental and instrumental change through mobilized, strategic prayer unlike anyone else in America. If you want to unlock the power of prayer to change the world, you must hear what Dave has to say because he is doing it! His insight on the link between covenant and authority is powerful. I love and respect him as a friend and catalyst in the worldwide prayer movement.

—*Pastor Geoff Eckart*
Chairman, National Prayer Committee
Lead Pastor, Daybreak Church, Grand Rapids, MI

David and the incredible work that he has pioneered through Intercessors for America. Within these pages, you will find marching orders for the reformers who are being raised up—the ones who will answer the call to both prayer and action. Now is your time to join ranks with these reformers to bring transformation to your family, to your city, and, ultimately, to your nation!

—*Ché Ahn, DMin*
Senior Leader, Harvest Rock Church, Pasadena, CA
President, Harvest International Ministry
International Chancellor, Wagner University

In *Impacting Generations*, David Kubal powerfully unpacks covenant history and what it means for us today. He clarifies that God's call and desire to bless nations isn't just in the past—we must step into it right now. This book is for anyone who wants to understand how prayer and action can shape the future. If you've ever wondered what it really means to "possess the gates," this book will open your eyes and challenge you to step up.

—*Matt Lockett*
Executive Director, Justice House of Prayer DC, Washington, DC

DAVID KUBAL

HOW ORDINARY PEOPLE CAN INFLUENCE THE FUTURE OF NATIONS

IMPACTING GENERATIONS

WHITAKER HOUSE

Unless otherwise indicated, all Scripture quotations are taken from the *New King James Version*, © 1979, 1980, 1982 by Thomas Nelson, Inc. Used by permission. All rights reserved. Scripture quotations marked (NLT) are taken from the *Holy Bible, New Living Translation*, © 1996, 2004, 2007 by Tyndale House Foundation. Used by permission of Tyndale House Publishers, Inc., Carol Stream, Illinois 60188. All rights reserved. Scripture quotations marked (NIV) are taken from the *Holy Bible, New International Version*®, NIV®, © 1973, 1978, 1984, 2011 by Biblica, Inc.® Used by permission of Zondervan. All rights reserved worldwide. www.zondervan.com. The "NIV" and "New International Version" are trademarks registered in the United States Patent and Trademark Office by Biblica, Inc.® Scripture quotations marked (AMPC) are taken from the *Amplified® Bible* Copyright © 1954, 1958, 1962, 1964, 1965, 1987 by The Lockman Foundation Used by permission. lockman.org. All rights reserved. Scripture quotations marked (MSG) are taken from *The Message: The Bible in Contemporary Language* by Eugene H. Peterson, © 1993, 1994, 1995, 1996, 2000, 2001, 2002. Used by permission of NavPress Publishing Group. All rights reserved. Represented by Tyndale House Publishers, Inc.

Boldface type in the Scripture quotations indicates the author's emphasis.

IMPACTING GENERATIONS
How Ordinary People Can Influence the Future of Nations

David Kubal
https://ifapray.org/
ifa@ifapray.org

ISBN: 979-8-88769-391-0
eBook ISBN: 979-8-88769-392-7
Printed in the United States of America
© 2025 by Intercessors for America

Whitaker House
1030 Hunt Valley Circle
New Kensington, PA 15068
www.whitakerhouse.com

Library of Congress Control Number: 2025901721

No part of this book may be reproduced or transmitted in any form or by any means, electronic or mechanical—including photocopying, recording, or by any information storage and retrieval system—without permission in writing from the publisher. Please direct your inquiries to permissionseditor@whitakerhouse.com.

CONTENTS

Foreword 9
Acknowledgments 13
Introduction 15

SECTION 1: A THEOLOGY OF NATIONS

1. The Lost Covenant 21
2. What Does It Mean to Possess the Gates? 29
3. Blessing the Nations 35
4. Prayer and the Sovereignty of God 41
5. Intercession Is Not Prayer 47
6. The Importance of Listening for Instruction 55
7. The True Nature of Humanity 61
8. Knowing Your Authority 67
9. The Necessity of Resilience 73

SECTION 2: ORDINARY PEOPLE, EXTRAORDINARY CALLINGS

    10. Victory at the Gate 81

    11. The Most Important Day in American History 89

    12. Prayer and Action Make a Difference 99

    13. Protecting the Vulnerable 107

    14. Intercession for Those in Authority 113

    15. Blessing Leaders Blesses the Nation 119

    16. Standing for Christ, Losing Popularity 125

SECTION 3: EXPLOITING SIN FOR CULTURAL CHANGE

    17. Return to the Tower of Babel 137

    18. Modern-Day Towers of Babel 143

SECTION 4: WHERE ARE WE HEADING?

    19. Global Crescendo of Freedom 155

    20. God's Design for Government 159

    21. Having Hope in the End Times 165

About the Author 173

FOREWORD

Nothing is more powerful or exhilarating than seeking the Lord and hearing His voice. So, the question must be asked, "How do mortal men and women hear from the Lord?"

In his new book, *Impacting Generations: How Ordinary People Can Influence the Future of Nations*, Dave Kubal answers that question: it is through prayer and intercession. Dave explains that there is a significant difference between the two.

The book opens the believer's eyes to the unimaginable power God has given His people to "possess the gates" of influence in a nation at all levels of government—local, state, national—and even internationally.

God works through His surrendered people to change society and come into alignment with His biblical plans for blessing. When God's people pray and intercede intentionally according to the holy Scriptures, then the supernatural power of the Holy Spirit comes into play, as history records, and people's lives are changed—then a nation is changed.

Dave's life is dedicated to motivating believers in Jesus Christ to pray and intercede. As the leader of Intercessors for America, Dave has brought together men and women who care about others and who know that the greatest change results from the internal change available to anyone who believes in the God of the Bible, confesses their sins, and surrenders their life to Jesus Christ.

No one's righteousness comes from good works. The Bible records in Genesis that Abraham's belief in God and surrender of his will in favor of God's will were accounted to Abraham as righteousness.

Dave Kubal lays out the covenants of God from Noah to Abraham. He wants the reader to understand the power available today through the Abrahamic covenant. Abraham's life was wholly surrendered to the will of God because he trusted and believed the promises God made to him to the point of following God's instruction to sacrifice his son Isaac on an altar. We know that an angel halted the sacrifice and provided a substitute (see Genesis 22:16–18). Abraham held God's favor because, in life, he demonstrated he had given everything he held dear to follow the voice of God in obedience. In return, God promised to bless trustworthy Abraham with unlimited descendants, and these descendants were promised they would "possess the gates of their enemies."

In addition, *all nations* of the earth would be blessed through Abraham's descendants because Abraham obeyed God's voice.

Therein lies the key for believers today. As believers who are children of Abraham (either naturally or grafted in), we can possess the gates of our enemies and thereby bless our nation!

Believers, it is time to stop being passive in the face of societal evil. It is time to possess the gates of the enemy and watch the Lord transform our nation with His unlimited blessing. Abraham was an ordinary man, made extraordinary by his complete surrender to the will of God.

You are no different. You can change the direction of your nation when you pray according to the Scripture, by faith, possess the gates of the enemy, and bring life-giving transformation to your nation.

That is God's plan. He does this powerful work through the power of the Holy Spirit. We do not do the transformation; He does, but God uses our faith and trust, as He did with Abraham, to bless the world.

—Michele Bachmann, JD, LLM
Former United States Representative
Dean, The Robertson School of Government, Regent University,
Virginia Beach, VA

ACKNOWLEDGMENTS

Special thanks to Kris Kubal, Judy McDonough, Kim Potter, Nicole Arnold-Bik, Rich Swingle, Nancy Huff, Cara Vest, and Keith Guinta.

INTRODUCTION

Embedded in the ancient Scriptures of the Old Testament is a promise and a command that will change the course of a nation. Followers of Christ and citizens worldwide are perplexed and overwhelmed by the need to find solutions to national problems. An answer is found in God's Word. It has become increasingly clear that we believers are destined to impact generations.

Each of us comes to this moment in time from our own unique perspective. Some have faith in a great revival that will impact the church and spill into the streets. Many are committed to "restoring the seven mountains of culture," inserting godly leaders in leadership positions to influence major cultural centers. Some people are convinced that we need the correct elected official(s) to be in place to make things right.

Hope for America ebbs and flows. Followers of Christ fluctuate from giving up on America to entertaining restrained optimism. It seems to me the vast majority are discouraged and overwhelmed by the complexity of the challenges our nation faces. A regular diet of news that focuses on negativity drags our spirits down daily. We're so accustomed to negative news that it's hard to believe a news outlet focused on positive stories could be relevant in our culture.

The solution to this has been hidden in plain sight for centuries. Before the gospel spread across the earth, before Jesus died for our sins, before the fall of Israel, and before the Israelites' forty-year journey, God made a promise to Abraham that is still in effect today. (See Genesis 12:1–3.)

This ancient promise God made to Abraham has the power to orchestrate God's greatest move in history. I believe we are entering a time when God's activity will be unmistakable and undeniable.

This book offers a fresh vision and understanding of our calling to impact our nations. When we understand God's promise and command to Abraham, we will find new hope for our positive influence in every level of society: HOAs, local communities, cities, counties, and state and federal jurisdictions. All of this is for a singular purpose: to bless nations.

Believers embedded within the American church are destined to make a difference. Before the creation of the universe, God had in His heart a strategy to position just the right people living in the US at this time in order to see His plans and purposes fulfilled.

God is not caught off guard by circumstances or the problems of the day. His plan is to use ordinary people like you and me to fulfill extraordinary callings. It is time to stop waiting for somebody else to do something! It is time for us to activate this ancient promise in our lives.

I can tell you that this movement has already started. There is a mighty wave of ordinary people accomplishing extraordinary feats. These people have determined they will no longer wait on somebody else to start something; they are going to do it themselves. These people have decided that what they felt led to do was not insignificant, so they made the first move. That move led to another and another. You will learn about many of these people in this book.

God's heart for His creation has always been to bless us with His love and mercy. He has promised this throughout time and displayed it in Scripture. The most exciting part of His plan is He desires to use us. His promise and His power are for us. You will see in this book you are destined to *Impact Generations*.

SECTION 1:

A THEOLOGY OF NATIONS

ONE

THE LOST COVENANT

Since my youth, I've been captivated by the profound mysteries of existence. Is there a God? How did the universe come into being? What is it made of? I viewed time as an enigma, with the past just a moment ago, the future a few seconds away, and the present unfolding in the now. If there is a God, has He revealed Himself to His creation? If so, does He care about us and the lives we lead?

As a teenager, I felt a gut-wrenching sense of purposelessness, so I sought answers to these questions. My youth pastor at church, a guy named Mike, taught me the historical nature of the books of the Bible. I delved into and discovered the story of Jesus, who claimed to be the Son of God. Not entirely convinced, I threw out a test: "God, if You are real, come in and change my life."

I was expecting fireworks, angelic appearances, and the like. Instead, I got an immediate and growing sense of purpose. I remember learning about Scriptures like Ephesians 2:10, which taught me that God created me with a specific purpose to do good works that He prepared in advance for me to do. This revelation was truly incredible!

This journey of discovery and faith transformed me from a lost and aimless teenager into a fervent seeker of God's plan for my life.

During this time, I was introduced to the concept of God's covenants. These are the pivotal moments in history when God the Father intervened in the human story to reveal His heart and establish a sacred pact. The significance of these covenants cannot be overstated, as they form the backbone of our shared spiritual journey.

Most of us would acknowledge that we serve a God of covenant, but do we understand His covenants well? Do we know which ones have been fulfilled and which have not? The Bible describes five covenants God made with man: the Noahic covenant (see Genesis 8:20–9:17), the Abrahamic covenant (see Genesis 12:1–3), the Mosaic covenant (see Exodus 19–24), the Davidic covenant (see 2 Samuel 7:8–29), and the New Covenant (see Jeremiah 31:31–34).

> *We live in a time that requires God's people to have a fresh understanding of the covenants He has made with us.*

Only with this new understanding will we have the confidence and hope to face the spiritual battles of the day. Let's take a look at these covenants.

THE NOAHIC COVENANT

In Genesis chapter 4, the Bible describes the sin and wickedness that had spread worldwide. Imagine, if you can, a world filled with such evil and wickedness, such sin, that only *one* family in the world *"found grace"* (Genesis 6:8) in the eyes of God. Noah was the only exception of righteousness. (See Genesis 6:5–9.)

With evil running rampant, justice demanded a response from God. God released a flood upon the earth unlike anything seen before. This flood destroyed the people and the corruption—except for Noah and his family, who alone were spared. After the flood, Noah built an altar and sacrificed to God. The smell of the soothing sacrifice was pleasing to God. (See Genesis 8:20–21.) Then and there, God swore He would never again destroy the earth with a flood:

> *And as for Me, behold, I establish My covenant with you and with your descendants after you, and with every living creature that is with you: the birds, the cattle, and every beast of the earth with you, of all that go out of the ark, every beast of the earth. Thus I establish My covenant with you: Never again shall all flesh be cut off by the waters of the flood; never again shall there be a flood to destroy the earth.*
>
> (Genesis 9:9–11)

This promise, the Noahic covenant, has stood firm to this day. This covenant is God's promise that He will *not* do something: He will not destroy humankind again.

THE MOSAIC COVENANT

The Mosaic covenant is unlike the Noahic covenant in that it is conditional, based on rewards for obedience and dire consequences for disobedience. This covenant was given to Moses at Mount Sinai. (See Exodus 19–24.) It is also known as "the Law." It consists of the Ten Commandments and other moral and civil laws. Jesus Christ fulfilled and replaced this covenant with the New covenant. The Mosaic covenant is no longer enforced and serves as the backdrop for the New covenant.

THE DAVIDIC COVENANT

The Davidic covenant was established through the line of David, which is the supremacy of Christ forever. (See 2 Samuel 7.) God is supreme on the throne, and His supremacy will always exist. This unconditional covenant promised that the line of King David would be blessed eternally with a kingdom that would never end. God spoke this to David through Nathan, the prophet. He said that David would not build a house for God but that his offspring would. David's kingdom, this covenant, would be established forever. God promised that His steadfast love would always be with the descendants of David. (See 2 Samuel 7:12–16.) Just like the Mosaic covenant, this covenant was fulfilled through the kingly line of Jesus Christ. It was, indeed, fulfilled at the cross of Christ. (See Mark 10:47.) The Davidic covenant no longer needs to be enforced. Jesus is on the throne.

THE NEW COVENANT

The New covenant is fulfilled in Jesus Christ, having been ratified through the shedding of Christ's blood. His death paid for our sins and fulfilled the covenant, causing the New covenant to spring forth once and forever. The Lord spoke about this future covenant through the prophet Jeremiah. Although the law was given and written on stone tablets, the Lord promised that, one day, He would put it in our minds and write it on our hearts. (See Jeremiah 31:31–34.) The book of Hebrews explains the New covenant and how it was established in Jesus, fulfilling the Mosaic and Davidic covenants. (See Hebrews 8:13; 12:24.)

THE LOST COVENANT OF ABRAHAM

The covenant that seems to have been lost in our day with virtually no understanding within the body of Christ, is the Abrahamic covenant. To be spiritual warriors in our day, we *must* understand the significance of this covenant and how it differs from the others.

We first read about the Abrahamic covenant in Genesis 12, immediately after the story of the Tower of Babel (the importance of Babel will be discussed later in chapter nineteen). Here is the scriptural description of this covenant:

> Now the LORD had said to Abram: "Get out of your country, from your family and from your father's house, to a land that I will show you. I will make you a great nation; I will bless you and make your name great; and you shall be a blessing. I will bless those who bless you, and I will curse him who curses you; and in you all the families of the earth shall be blessed." (Genesis 12:1–3)

So, Abraham left his land and traveled to where God showed him. The relationship between God and Abraham was based on mutual commitments. As Abraham obeyed God's instruction, God provided supplies and land so that he would become a great nation, even though he had no offspring then.

Abraham continued to follow the Lord's instructions over the decades. Due to Abraham's faithfulness, the Lord expanded the covenant a few times. The final, culminating version of this covenant is found in Genesis 22. The Bible tells us that God tested Abraham. God said, "Take now your son, your only son Isaac, whom you love, and go to the land of Moriah, and offer him there as a burnt offering on one of the mountains of which I shall tell you" (Genesis 22:2).

Once again, Abraham obeyed God. He took his son to the mountain God had specified and prepared to sacrifice him. As he drew back the knife to kill his only son, an angel of the Lord spoke to him, stopping him from sacrificing his promise, saying, "*Do not lay your hand on the lad, or do anything to him; for now I know that you fear God, since you have not withheld your son, your only son, from Me*" (Genesis 22:12). Abraham looked up and saw a ram, which he then sacrificed instead. (See Genesis 22:13.) It's easy to imagine his relief.

At this point, the Lord repeated His covenant promise to Abraham but made a critical addition:

> *By Myself I have sworn, says the* Lord, *because you have done this thing, and have not withheld your son, your only son—blessing I will bless you, and multiplying I will multiply your descendants as the stars of the heaven and as the sand which is on the seashore; and your descendants shall possess the gate of their enemies. In your seed all the nations of the earth shall be blessed, because you have obeyed My voice.* (Genesis 22:16–18)

Abraham's obedient step of faith positioned him to receive this final phase of God's covenant with him. The Lord had promised to bless Abraham greatly through his descendants and to make them a great nation. He had vowed to align Himself with Abraham and his descendants in blessings and curses. He added, "*Your descendants shall possess the gate of their enemies. In your seed all the nations of the earth shall be blessed*" (verses 17–18).

> **We are destined to impact generations.**

Think about this for a moment. The Noahic covenant is an ongoing covenant for God not to do something—that is, destroy the earth with a flood. The Mosaic and Davidic covenants are fulfilled in Christ. The

New Covenant provides forgiveness for our sins through Christ and eternally establishes Him on the throne.

There is one covenant that is unique and stands out among them all: the Abrahamic covenant. Why? *Because it continues to be fulfilled as an ongoing covenant. It is both being fulfilled and yet to be fulfilled.*

We know that the descendants of Abraham include all believers in Christ who are grafted into the family of God. (See Romans 11; Galatians 3.) God has promised that His people, the descendants of Abraham by faith, will possess the enemy's gates and be a blessing for all nations.

But what does "possessing the gates" mean? How will this covenant be fulfilled? What is our part to play? The Abrahamic covenant, which is yet to be fulfilled, is a governmental mandate given to us centuries ago. God wants us to fulfill it. Today, He wants us to fulfill this covenant promise of possessing our enemy's gates, blessing all nations, and impacting generations.

The Hebrew verb *"possess"* in Genesis 22:17 is in the present imperative tense, which means it is ongoing. This covenant of God is at work now and will continue into the future. It hasn't arrived, and it hasn't yet been completed. It is up to us to help fulfill this covenant promise.

We must have a renewed understanding of how the Abrahamic covenant applies to us and how it can be fulfilled through us. We are not only called to bless nations, but God *wants* us to bless nations. God's only ongoing covenant with humanity is for us to influence seats of authority to bring His blessing to the earth.

> *God wants us to bless nations, God calls us to bless nations, and God empowers us to bless nations.*

To do that, we must first possess the gates of our enemy.

TWO

WHAT DOES IT MEAN TO POSSESS THE GATES?

Possessing the enemy's gates is not a military coup or a violent overthrow of the present government. It is a spiritual concept rooted in the societal culture of early Bible times. It means to ideologically influence the policies of communities, cities, states, and nations.

In Genesis 22, in a remarkable and foundational covenant, God assured Abraham that his descendants would possess the gates of their enemies and be a blessing to nations—not only Abraham and his physical descendants but also those of us who are spiritual descendants of Abraham. This covenant promise empowers us with a profound sense of responsibility and purpose, a duty to uphold, and a role to play in the grand narrative of God's plan concerning nations. We are not mere spectators but active participants in the unfolding of this promise.

In the Old Testament, the gates of a city held immense significance and served many purposes. The gate was part of a prominent physical structure that protected and defended from invasion. It was also an entry and exit point, so allegiances were verified at the city gate. The gate was also a place of authority, where city rulers established policies and laws. City government was conducted at the gates. It was there that leaders established the city's ideological thoughts, values, and ideas.

Certain people were permitted to pass through the gates in those days, while certain others were prohibited. When someone was granted entry, they had to submit to the rules of the city they were entering. Ultimately, the gates were a place to establish and exert control. If a ruler did not control the gates of his city, he would have no control over the city or what happened within its walls.

> You must control the gates in order to control the city.

Gates are mentioned many times in the Bible. Proverbs 1 tells us that wisdom sits at the gates of the city, which means that the decisions and policies made at the gates should be guided by wisdom.

The gate was the entry point for welcoming or warding off visitors. At the gate of Sodom, Lot greeted the angels who came before they destroyed the city. (See Genesis 19:1.)

The gate was a place for the community to receive help from the city leadership. According to Moses's laws, parents were required to bring their rebellious children to the city gates, where leaders would assess the children and pronounce judgment on them. (See Deuteronomy 21:18–21.)

Legal matters were decided at the city gates. Boaz assumed the role of kinsman/redeemer by engaging with the elders at the gate of Bethlehem. (See Ruth 4:1–12.)

News was shared at the gates. In 1 Samuel 4, Eli, the priest, waited at the gate to find out the result of a battle.

King David cared for government affairs at the gates. (See 2 Samuel 18–19.)

Political intrigue occurred at the gates. In Esther 2, Mordecai overheard a plot to assassinate the king at the gate.

The significance of the gates of cities continued in the time of Christ, which helps us understand His statement to Peter in Matthew 16 that the gates of hell would not prevail against the church. (See verse 18.) This declaration echoes the promise God made to Abraham and proclaims that in the authority of Christ, believers will fulfill His plan for the church. Power and authority lie within the gates. Jesus was declaring that Satan would not defeat the church nor have authority over God's people. Instead, the church, the body of Christ, will possess the gates of our enemies, including the gates of hell, and see a fulfillment of the covenant God made to Abraham.

Knowing the role of gates in those times helps us understand the import of God's promise to Abraham in Genesis 22:17: *"Your descendants will possess the gate of their enemies."* This was not meant to describe a literal possession of physical gates but a metaphorical concept of gaining authority, influence, and control over the enemy's territory. Control of the gates means control of entire cities.

Someone always possesses the gates of authority. The leadership of a city or a nation determines the laws and values, but even in a vacuum of leadership, there will be those who step in to control.

For Christians, who are the descendants of Abraham, possessing the gates is not about a human lust for power. By possessing the gates,

Abraham's descendants will bless all nations and impact generations as God's values sweep across humanity. We possess the gates by influencing the government's ideologies, policies, regulations, laws, and values, bringing God's kingdom to this earth.

Though the Scriptures refer to the gates in many different ways, only two Scriptures state that we are commanded to possess them. We have already discussed Genesis 22. The other passage occurs two chapters later, in Genesis 24. However, to understand the significance of this second command to possess the gates, we must understand what happened in Genesis 23.

Genesis 23 spans forty years. During those forty years, Abraham and his family experienced difficulties. Abraham lost his beautiful wife, Sarah; their son of promise, Isaac, remained unmarried until near the age of forty. God's promise to Abraham—that his descendants would be as numerous as the grains of sand on the seashore—seemed more unlikely by the hour. God had told Abraham that his descendants would possess the gates of their enemy, yet he had only one descendant. How would this promise come to pass?

Abraham devised a divine plan with a specific strategy. He sent a servant to travel over 500 miles and convince a stranger to marry his son Isaac. Abraham knew he needed someone who could hear God's voice and seek God's face for direction along the way. He needed an intercessor.

The man Abraham chose for this assignment embarked upon his journey and rode a camel for weeks to arrive at his destination. He felt impressed by the Lord to stop at a specific watering hole in Abraham's home country and make his camels kneel by the well. As they rested, he prayed:

O Lord God of my master Abraham, please give me success this day, and show kindness to my master Abraham. Behold, here I stand by the well of water, and the daughters of the city's men are coming out to draw water. Now let it be that the young woman to whom I say, "Please let down your pitcher that I may drink," and she says, "Drink, and I will also give your camels a drink"—let her be the one You have appointed for Your servant Isaac. And by this I will know that You have shown kindness to my master.

(Genesis 24:12–14)

The next verse should encourage all of us who pray. Genesis 24:15 says, *"Before he had finished speaking,…Rebekah…came out with her pitcher on her shoulder"* (Genesis 24:15). Before he even finished praying, Rebekah entered the picture.

Eventually, the servant/intercessor visited Rebekah's house and explained his mission to her family. He recounted how he had prayed. He shared how she had come out and offered him and his camels water. He told them about the God of his master, Abraham, and how exponentially God had blessed him. Surely, these people had heard of this friend of God. Then, he asked if they would allow Rebekah to go with him. Miraculously, Rebekah and her family said yes.

However, that is not the greatest miracle.

As Rebekah prepared to leave, her family placed their hands on her to bless her. This was their blessing: *"May you become the mother of thousands of ten thousands; and may your descendants possess the gates of those who hate them"* (Genesis 24:60). This impromptu, unchoreographed blessing confirms the *exact* blessing God promised Abraham four decades earlier. Rebekah's family and the servant/intercessor played a crucial role in confirming the covenant promise God had given Abraham. I can imagine that the servant knew about God's promise and was sure the Lord had led him to Rebekah when he heard the blessing.

That day, supernatural activity revealed that God's purposes were divinely set in motion by a man of prayer. The servant's prayer enabled him to discern God's direction. Most important, his intercession activated past covenantal promises from decades earlier and released blessings for generations of nations.

Perhaps you are reading this and wondering about the promises God has made to you in the past few months or even decades. You question if you heard God right. He seemed to confirm the promises, yet nothing has happened. God is faithful to His promises. You will see a performance of the things spoken to you by the Lord. Don't give up. Intercession will tip the bowls and bring them to a place of attainment at the right time.

THREE

BLESSING THE NATIONS

God promised Abraham that his descendants would possess the gates and bless the nations. What is God's heart for the nations? If we are to possess the gates of our cities and nations, we must first understand God's heart for nations, for it is the firm foundation on which we stand.

FIRST, GOD ESTABLISHES NATIONS

A nation's birth or demise is not brought about by mere chance or circumstance. It is the divine work of our eternal, all-powerful Father, who, in His wisdom, allows the interplay of good and evil forces to work in a nation.

It has been said: "The church gets the government it deserves." This profound truth is a testament to how God employs those who strive for righteousness to mold our nations.

> *He makes nations great, and destroys them;*
> *He enlarges nations, and guides them.*
> *(Job 12:23)*

SECOND, GOD ESTABLISHES THE BORDERS AND THE PLACES FOR US TO LIVE

As humanity cooperates with God's sovereign hand over time, His borders are established. These borders define the boundaries of the nations we are to live in, and Scripture even says that God sets the time for us to live. This should fill us with profound hope and purpose today. God has determined both when and where we live in this challenging time:

> *And He has made from one blood every nation of men to dwell on all the face of the earth, and has determined their preappointed times and the boundaries of their dwellings, so that they should seek the Lord, in the hope that they might grope for Him and find Him, though He is not far from each one of us.* (Acts 17:26–27)

THIRD, EVERY NATION IN THE WORLD HAS THE POTENTIAL TO BE AN EXCEPTIONAL NATION

Like many in other nations, I, as an American, consider my nation exceptional. The view that greatness is possible in a nation enables praying citizens to have a vision to possess the gates—to pray for, intercede for, and work for God's best for their nation.

God's purposes and our actions are linked. In the eighteenth chapter of Jeremiah, we find a famous passage in which God uses the word picture of a potter and his clay to illustrate His ways of working in our lives. The potter takes a marred piece of clay and reworks it into a vessel that the potter thinks is good. But what most people don't realize is that the Lord immediately relates this illustration to how He works with nations:

> *The instant I speak concerning a nation and concerning a kingdom, to pluck up, to pull down, and to destroy it, if that nation against whom I have spoken turns from its evil, I will relent of the disaster that I thought to bring upon it. And the instant I speak concerning a nation and concerning a kingdom, to build and to plant it, if it does evil in My sight so that it does not obey My voice, then I will relent concerning the good with which I said I would benefit it.*
> (Jeremiah 18:7–10)

God's heart for every nation is a positive outcome, which He calls "*good*" in this passage. God's will is for every nation—whether it be the United States, France, Iran, Russia, Gambia, or another nation—is positive and exceptional. He calls all nations into being and warns them if they get off track. This theological concept is complex for twenty-first-century followers of Christ to accept. So I ask: why would God create a nation that is doomed? Does He not offer the opportunity, the grace, the vehicle of national repentance for a nation to align with His purposes? This passage makes it clear: the outcome depends on the decisions made by a nation and its leaders, whether they do good or evil in the eyes of the Lord. "*Blessed is the nation whose God is the LORD*" (Psalm 33:12).

FOURTH, GOD HOLDS NATIONS AND THEIR CITIZENS ACCOUNTABLE

Just as God holds each person accountable for their personal decisions, He holds nations accountable for their collective decisions. We are not exempt from blame for any poor decisions our nation's leaders make. In Micah 5:15 (NLT), the Lord declares, "*I will pour out my vengeance on all the nations that refuse to obey me.*"

FIFTH, A REPRESENTATIVE REPUBLIC IS GOD'S DESIGN FOR GOVERNMENT

This pattern is found in Exodus 18, where Moses's father-in-law, Jethro, offered Moses sage advice about how to organize a team to help him bear the responsibilities of leading the Israelites. Jethro recognized that it was not good for Moses to try to handle all the decision-making and judging alone. He suggested that Moses...

> ...*select from all the people able men, such as fear God, men of truth, hating covetousness; and place such over them to be rulers of thousands, rulers of hundreds, rulers of fifties, and rulers of tens. And let them judge the people at all times. Then it will be that every great matter they shall bring to you, but every small matter they themselves shall judge. So it will be easier for you, for they will bear the burden with you. If you do this thing, and God so commands you, then you will be able to endure, and all this people will also go to their place in peace.* (Exodus 18:21–23)

Then Moses did what Jethro suggested, creating a leadership team with four levels of authority. Whatever they couldn't handle—the "hard cases"—they brought to Moses, but everything else they took care of. Each tribe would have leaders and judges who would apply the law of God, with Moses judging the most challenging issues.

This design of divvied-up governmental duties is the genesis of the global freedoms we see today. The United States is one of many representative republics patterned after the Old Testament government.

Finally, we look at the results of a good government: religious freedom. This truth is found in 1 Timothy 2:1–4:

> *Therefore I exhort first of all that supplications, prayers, intercessions, and giving of thanks be made for all men, for kings and all*

who are in authority, that we may lead a quiet and peaceable life in all godliness and reverence. For this is good and acceptable in the sight of God our Savior, who desires all men to be saved and to come to the knowledge of the truth.

The hallmark of good government is religious freedom. Paul states in this passage that we should pray for *"a quiet and peaceable life"* so that God's desire to see *"all men...saved"* will be achieved. Religious freedoms that allow the gospel to go forth are the preeminent conclusion of what "good government" is.

The religious freedoms Americans enjoy have enabled our nation to produce more Christian missionaries and invest more dollars in kingdom endeavors than any nation in history. None of this could be accomplished apart from intercession for religious freedom. Many are called to bring kingdom values to service in the public arena, and, for that, we are thankful. However, even if we are not called to public service, we are still called to pray that our leaders would allow us to worship our God as we desire to.

A commonly held view today is that the government has nothing to do with God and is a manufactured institution created by those seeking power to control. Government is often viewed as a necessary evil to keep civilization from imploding.

> *The biblical truth of the matter is that government is divine. God created it for His purposes.*

God has a design for good government in His heart for every nation. The Bible teaches:

1. God establishes nations.
2. God establishes the borders and who should live in them.
3. Every nation has the potential to be exceptional.
4. God holds nations accountable.
5. A representative republic is God's design for government.
6. Religious freedom is the ultimate indicator of good government.

FOUR

PRAYER AND THE SOVEREIGNTY OF GOD

God calls us to impact generations, but is that really something we can do?

Some people believe God created the universe and that all of us and all of history—future and past—are a part of His unfolding plan. Is His plan on autopilot so that we are mere passengers along for the ride?

This view often sounds like this: if God controls everything, why should I be involved in my community? I go to church and walk uprightly with God. Why should we pray? God is going to do what He wants. Why should I vote or be involved in politics?

This view concludes that God is not God if He is not in charge, so He must have his way. He will accomplish His will.

I often hear this from people who have looked at circumstances and are overwhelmed. They have resigned themselves to the idea that they cannot do anything to affect their nation and are not responsible for any outcomes.

This thinking results in the triumph of evil and accepts less than God's best for us. Evil will triumph if good people sit idly by.

Some Scriptures reinforce the view that we are not in control, including the following:

> *The king's heart is in the hand of the LORD, like the rivers of water; He turns it wherever He wishes.* (Proverbs 21:1)

Yet, when Jesus was asked by His disciples how to pray, He replied that we should pray the following:

> *Our Father in heaven, hallowed be Your name. Your kingdom come. Your will be done on earth as it is in heaven.* (Luke 11:2)

Other Scriptures clearly state that God controls the destiny of nations—for example, "God reigns over the nations; God sits on his holy throne" (Psalm 47:8).

Still, Jesus reminds us to continue to ask for justice:

> *Will not God bring about justice for his chosen ones, who cry out to him day and night? Will he keep putting them off?* (Luke 18:7 NIV)

Gatekeepers and intercessors with a heart to impact generations must answer this question: does God reign, or is history left to us? Without a clear answer, we will be confused and will constantly question God.

Three types of verses within Scripture clarify this question. Some Scriptures explain God's:

1. Sovereignty
2. Perfect will
3. Permissive will

Correctly understanding the relationship between these types of Scriptures will explain and empower followers of Christ to impact generations.

GOD'S SOVEREIGNTY

God's sovereignty is the understanding that God is the supreme ruler of the universe and has the right and ability to do whatever He wants, whenever He wants. Nothing happens without His direction or permission, and He is not bound or limited by His creatures. God's sovereignty is a biblical teaching that affirms His authority over all things.

God is certainly in charge of everything. He is working out His plan for humanity, and His ultimate plan will come to pass through His sovereign will.

This doctrine is taught through verses such as the following:

But our God is in heaven; He does whatever He pleases.
(Psalm 115:3)

I know that You can do everything, and that no purpose of Yours can be withheld from You. (Job 42:2)

There are many plans in a man's heart, nevertheless the Lord's counsel—that will stand. (Proverbs 19:21)

God does reign. His perfect will for us concerns His plans and destinies for each person.

> *For I know the thoughts that I think toward you, says the* Lord, *thoughts of peace and not of evil, to give you a future and a hope.*
>
> (Jeremiah 29:11)

> *For we are His workmanship, created in Christ Jesus for good works, which God prepared beforehand that we should walk in them.*
>
> (Ephesians 2:10)

GOD'S PERFECT WILL

Scriptures concerning God's perfect will for our lives bring comfort and peace. We know that God is sovereign and good and has good things in His heart for us. His perfect will for each of us is eternal and cannot be changed or destroyed. His heart for us, His will for our lives, His destinies never alter. His perfect will for us is perfect.

However, God's sovereignty needs to be understood within the context of free will. His sovereign decision to allow us to make our own decisions creates a path that differs from His perfect will.

GOD'S PERMISSIVE WILL

God permits us to choose how we lead our lives. God's permissive will allows for free will and our ability to choose freely. God's permissive will allows us to make good, bad, and even evil choices—it is up to us.

(There is much theological debate on the extent of our free choices: our ability to choose salvation, our ability to go against God's perfect will for people, and so on. We must recognize this debate, but this book is not meant to settle the debate, only to point out we have free will.)

He has given us free will to choose: *"For this is the will of God, that by doing good you may put to silence the ignorance of foolish men"* (1 Peter 2:15).

Even so, God can use any choice we make for His purposes: *"And we know that all things work together for good to those who love God, to those who are the called according to His purpose"* (Romans 8:28).

God's *permissive* will permits us to choose our future and to decide whether we want to experience God's perfect will for us.

In summary, God is sovereign. His sovereign will includes His perfect will and His permissive will. We will be part of His sovereign will in one way or another—actively working toward His perfect will or passively experiencing His permissive will.

People wonder how there can be anything like God's perfect will in this sinful, broken world we live in. You might ask, "Doesn't sin affect everything, leaving us with God's second best?"

The answer is *yes*! This is the central point of God's sovereignty. His *perfect* plans and destinies for individuals and nations are eternally intact. What He *permits* is our choice to pursue—or not pursue—His *perfect* plan.

We constantly struggle for God's best for our lives, communities, and nations. It's all about restoration amid what He permits to pursue what is perfect. God's perfect will for our nation can still be realized when Christians influence policy—as we possess the gates and pray for God's best in His permissive will. Possessing the gates restores God's perfect will for a nation. Good government is the national restoration from sin.

> *Intercession ushers in God's perfect will, and as we pray,*
> *He redeems circumstances that result from*
> *His permissive will.*

You might say prayer brings in the best amid the bad as we intercede for His destiny. God will have His way in our nation because He is sovereign, but will it be His permissive will, or will it be steps toward His perfect will?

FIVE

INTERCESSION IS NOT PRAYER

Intercession is an intimidating word that is rarely used today. How often do you incorporate this word into your daily conversations? Let us review how this word was used in the Old and New Testaments.

Many Hebrew words in the Old Testament are interpreted as "prayer," "intercession," "praise," and "supplication." *Tephillah*, translated as "prayer," occurs more than seventy times. *Palal*, meaning "to pray," appears more than eighty times. In ten of those occurrences, it means "to intercede." Finally, *paga* occurs over fifty times and is translated as "intercede" four times.

The Old Testament concept of intercession generally revolves around one person intervening for the sake of others. Abraham interceded for Abimelech (see Genesis 20:17), God instructed Moses to have Aaron intercede for the Israelites (see Numbers 6:24–26), and Job interceded for his friends (see Job 42:8). The task of intercession was assigned to a minimal number of people on behalf of a large number of people.

Prayer was a general and accessible way for the common person to bring requests before God. The Old Testament concept of intercession is entirely different. Intercession was reserved for a select few with the critical task of standing between God and God's divine purposes for a person or nation. These intercessors would know God's heart and man's needs.

In the New Testament, intercession has a distinct meaning compared to prayer. Similar to the various Hebrew terms in the Old Testament, numerous Greek words in the New Testament are translated as "prayer," "supplication," and "intercession." However, the Greek term for intercession appears only *once* as a command. Many individuals involved in the prayer movement frequently use intercession interchangeably with prayer. Nevertheless, intercession differs from prayer.

To better understand this single scriptural command to be intercessors, let's first look at two words most frequently translated as "pray." These words are *proseuchomai*, which means "to pray," and *proseuché*, which means "prayer" or "a place for prayer." *Proseuchomai* is found eighty-six times in the New Testament; *proseuché*, thirty-eight times.

Both Greek terms are compound words with similar meanings. The first portion of *proseuchomai* is *pros*, a preposition meaning "motion toward a place." The second portion of the word, *euchomai*, means "pray to God."

Putting the meanings together shows us the literal sense: "prayer toward a specific goal." Jesus taught His disciples to pray—*proseuchomai*—toward an end goal. *"Your kingdom come. Your will be done"* (Matthew 6:10). Praying toward a goal is not bad. The New Testament encourages us to do this over a hundred times. We pray when we bring our needs before God. Prayer is bringing our needs to God. Nothing is wrong with this; we are commanded to pray without ceasing. (See 1 Thessalonians 5:17.)

Intercession is entirely different.

The word for "intercession" is used only five times in the New Testament. The Greek word is *entugchanó*. Four instances are general, and one is a command. Let's first look at the general usage in Romans 8:26: *"Likewise the Spirit also helps in our weaknesses. For we do not know what we should pray for as we ought, but the Spirit Himself makes intercession for us with groanings which cannot be uttered."*

This verse tells us the Spirit provides the opportunity for us to be involved in intercession. Intercession is now for everyone! The Holy Spirit makes intercession *through* us. Most people who read the verse think it is just the Holy Spirit who intercedes, but I believe the verse says the Holy Spirit's intercession creates *"groanings" within us.*

Intercession involves the Holy Spirit and the believer. Intercession is not just the work of the Holy Spirit. He directs and leads *us* in intercession. The term "Spirit-led prayer" is used very commonly. How does the Spirit lead us through groanings, impressions, leanings, senses, and so on? We can't always put words to it, but Spirit-led prayer is a deep understanding of where we are to go.

The Greek word translated *"groanings"* in Romans 8:26 is thought by some to refer to speaking in tongues. This is an incorrect understanding, as Paul does not use the word for speaking in tongues ("glossolalia") but rather the word *stenagmois*. This word is related to the English word stenography.

Commonly found in courtrooms, a stenographer quietly listens to what is being said and translates the spoken word into a written form. The gift of intercession given to all is the gift of listening to God, as a stenographer would, and translating that into prayers.

The other important point to glean from this verse is that intercession is now for the commoner. This must have been a mind-blowing concept to the religious class of Paul's day. At the time, the religious leaders were the only ones who could stand between God and the people. As important intermediaries, they had job security, authority, and self-worth. But Paul, in his theological treatise that is the book of Romans, blows away this exclusivity when he says the Spirit makes intercession with us as we groan. Anyone who has the Holy Spirit is now able to intercede.

Entugchanó, is the Greek word for "intercession." To correctly understand the Greek word for intercession, one must understand it as a consultation process in which two parties cooperate. In intercession, one comes looking for advice, and the other gives it. One has more power and authority than the other. We enter into the intercessory process with the Lord.

The root word of *entugchanó* is *tugchanó*, which means hitting the mark. It was an archery term. An archer would pull the arrow back and launch it, and if it hit the bullseye, it was *tugchanó*. We learn about one of the most fascinating aspects of this word for intercession by looking at the opposite word in Greek. *Hamartia* means "to *miss* the mark." The archer would pull back the arrow and launch it, and if it missed the bullseye, it was *hamartia*, translated into English as the word "sin"!

That's right: the opposite of sin is intercession. Through sin, we miss the mark; through intercession, we hit the mark. Intercession is a critical part of the process of restoration of sin. Let's put all of this together: intercession is a consultation process that we follow in order to hit the mark.

Intercessors:

- Seek first to understand the heart of God in a matter.
- Prioritize listening to the Holy Spirit before speaking.

- See themselves as vital instruments cooperating with God to release His perfect will.

- Humbly come before God, desiring to hit the mark by cooperating with Him.

- Ask God what His divine purposes are for a person, a situation, or a nation.

- Sit at the intersection between God's divine will and men, crying out for His will to be done.

- Prayer is excellent; we are commanded to bring our needs before the Lord. But may I suggest the following?

- Prayer relates to God's permissive will. Intercession relates to God's perfect will.

- Prayer deals with circumstances. Intercession deals with divine purposes.

- Prayer involves a list. Intercession involves listening.

So, intercession is used in a general sense five times in the New Testament and only once as a command. Look at 1 Timothy 2:1–2:

> *Therefore I exhort first of all that supplications, prayers, intercessions, and giving of thanks be made for all men, for kings and all who are in authority, that we may lead a quiet and peaceable life in all godliness and reverence.*

Supplications and prayers are for those felt needs we ask for amid circumstances. However, intercession is about consulting with God to hit the mark of our requests and release divine destiny. Intercession restores God's perfect will, while prayer is our list of felt needs resulting from living amid God's permissive will.

> *We are to intercede with our spirits and pray with our minds.*

We can miss the presence of God through prayer alone, but we cannot intercede without experiencing the presence of God.

I have learned something from years working with people who call themselves intercessors for America. It's not because we like to pray. We are intercessors for America because God commands us, first and foremost, to consult with Him about how we can release His destiny for our nation. Intercession is, first and foremost, a governmental activity. Intercession for the nation's leaders is prioritized in these critical verses from Paul's first letter to Timothy. Possessing the gates of the enemy is about influencing the centers of authority so that they will be restored to the best version of God's perfect will. Prayer is important, but we live in a day when we must intercede. To truly bless our communities, states, and nation, we must cooperate with the Holy Spirit in intercession. Yet, it can be challenging for us to stop praying and start interceding.

I recently taught about the difference between prayer and intercession at a conference for intercessors. I asked the participants to put their teaching on intercession into practice. I asked them to listen and to ask the Lord what He would want to show them about their states, which is what we were praying about.

I stopped talking and waited while they followed my instructions. It was awkward for many of the attendees. Silence can be that way. Yet, after a few moments, about 80 percent of the attendees got it. Some, however, were unwilling or unable to stop sharing with God their lists and their diagnoses of what was wrong with their states.

After some time, I asked for reports of what God had revealed. One woman excitedly shared that she received clarity from the Lord like never before. Another told us that she immediately received a vision, a mental picture that illustrated a spiritual truth about her state.

However, there was one woman who didn't seem to understand at all. When we began to intercede together, she kept praying, asking the Lord to do one thing after another that came to her mind. It became uncomfortable as others who understood the assignment looked awkwardly at me.

The fact is, it can be uncomfortable to allow the silence that is necessary to hear from God. After all, we each know people who talk constantly and fill every pause in conversations. There is that same urge to do all the talking with God. Yet, we must ask Him to help us overcome our discomfort and our habits to mature in our relationship with Him.

At another conference, I led the same exercise. I asked the people to stop praying and to listen to God in intercession. Those in attendance became silent, listening for instruction from God. As before, it was awkward at first. After a few moments of silence, I asked if they had heard or seen anything. One woman shared that she saw a bag of potato chips. This may sound odd, but it is what she saw, and she was willing to step out in faith and share this vision.

She explained that a bag of chips is often only half full, or less than that, when you open it up, so you have only part of the bag, not a whole bag. She commented that she had no idea how to pray about this. Another woman quickly responded, declaring that she knew how to pray. She began to pray over their leadership that they would each be a "whole bag of chips," not coming up short.

It may take time for you to become comfortable making intercession a regular part of your prayer life. However, if you tune in to God, He will cause you to see from His perspective in a way you can understand so that you can pray more effectively. Praying through lists can be part of a robust spiritual life, especially when the list is developed and guided by the Holy Spirit. However, if we only pray lists, we will not experience the blessing of possessing the gates of our enemies. It is only when we submit and rest in our relationship with the Lord and look to Him for direction, as Abraham did, that our prayers will "hit the mark," and we will begin to intercede in ways that will be powerful and effective.

SIX

THE IMPORTANCE OF LISTENING FOR INSTRUCTION

Most intercessors recognize that part of their calling includes being an active watchman. The Old Testament teaches this principle in many places. According to the *Strong's Concordance*, a watchman keeps guard, observes, and gives heed. His job is to watch, to keep, to restrain, to preserve, protect, to keep within bounds, and to guard. With these insightful descriptions in mind, let's look at the book of Isaiah.

> *I have posted watchmen on your walls, Jerusalem; they will never be silent day or night. You who call on the* Lord, *give yourselves no rest, and give him no rest till he establishes Jerusalem and makes her the praise of the earth.* (Isaiah 62:6–7 NIV)

What vivid imagery this passage provides for intercessors. Picture this with me: We take our post on the wall of protection, surrounding those things we desire to see for our nation as we persistently cry out to God. We pray and intercede without ceasing until God's will is accomplished. We position ourselves, our hearts, and our minds to passionately pray, knowing God will accomplish His earthly purposes, just as He promised. Our positioning and persistent crying out are conduits of His mighty power. These practices—taking our position and making passionate pleas—are vital for a faithful watchman. However, I believe there is another critical requirement to being an effective watchman. Let's look at a couple of Scripture verses:

> *Son of man, I have made you a watchman for the people of Israel; so hear the word I speak and give them warning from me.*
> (Ezekiel 3:17 NIV)

> *I will stand at my watch and station myself on the ramparts; I will look to see what he will say to me, and what answer I am to give to this complaint.* (Habakkuk 2:1 NIV)

These two Scriptures emphasize hearing the voice and the Word of God. Often, watchmen emphasize looking at the horizon from their positions on the wall. They are diligent to remain up-to-date on the news. They constantly scroll through social media to keep apprised of what is happening in their area. They discuss current events with other intercessors. They participate in online prophetic communities that analyze the current state of affairs. They closely watch the horizon to see what is coming down the path. Yet, they are not always equally diligent about turning their gaze toward heaven for instruction. They may not be as persistent in asking the Lord to give them revelation and instruction as the Lord would have them be. God said to Habakkuk, "Write the vision and make it plain on tablets, that he may run who reads it" (Habakkuk 2:2).

Why is it more important to look to heaven than to the horizon for what is happening in our world? Here's why: Looking to heaven will ultimately cause your faith to grow immensely. If we focus on the troubles of the day and the enemies of God's kingdom warring against us, we are likely to become discouraged and dismayed. We may even be overwhelmed by the burden of intercession regarding events in our nation. We see this daily in the body of Christ—people are weary, and many are mentally spent.

The enemy of our souls seeks to discourage, disrupt, and demean our faith. Things change when we look to God with our focus fixed on Him, and He speaks His word to us for this present day. When He reveals His revelation and insight for this moment, your faith will surge exponentially. You will be empowered, and your intercession will be rejuvenated so that you recover your former passion. This is one of the ways we possess the gates of our enemies.

I have seen this happen many times in my life. In 2022, during the National Day of Prayer, I was walking along the Capitol grounds from one event to another when I saw the area called the Summerhouse. Part of an update to the Capitol grounds in the late 1800s, this area provides visitors with water and a place to rest. It has always fascinated me. I can imagine visitors of the Capitol and elected officials from years past bringing their horses for a drink from this natural, spring-fed well.

While walking that day, I noticed a repair project for the springs that flow under the Capitol grounds. I immediately heard the Lord speak to my spirit. He said, "The wellsprings of this nation are being drawn upon by godly leaders and are, in turn, restoring freedom and godly values."

God showed me that we are seeing physical evidence in the natural realm of what He is doing in the spiritual realm. He is repairing, restoring, and rebuilding the foundational springs that are welling up in our nation. God is restoring our nation's wellsprings. I later shared this word from God at an Intercessors for America event for the National Day of Prayer.

As only God could orchestrate, fellow intercessor Barbara Iuliano was watching and couldn't wait to pick up the phone and call our office. She connected with Amy Sabat, an IFA staff member, and excitedly shared a dream she had had several years ago. She knew this particular dream was from the Lord because it was so vivid. In it, she saw people walking through an archway and being healed. It didn't matter what the malady was—blindness, lameness, deafness, mental illness—they were healed. She had prayed into this dream for years, asking the Lord about it, especially regarding the arch's location. The very morning of the National Day of Prayer broadcast, she saw the arch again and *knew* the Lord was bringing healing as people passed through the archway. When she heard me talk about the wellsprings on the webcast and then saw the picture of the arch from her dream, it resonated in her spirit. She was confident this was the arch God had shown her in the dream.

After the webcast, Barbara inquired of the Lord about the project to repair the springs under the Capitol. She asked the Lord if that was a picture of Him bringing healing to the nation. I believed the answer was yes. Barbara shared with us that the arch was a symbol of passing through. As you know, we all go through the waters of tumultuous experiences to get to the other side. God is faithful; He always brings us through and into those clean, peaceful waters, and we experience purification, restoration, and healing.

The timing of this dream deeply moved me. The details would never have been shared if Barbara had not called the wrong line that day. That day was our nation's seventieth official National Day of Prayer. On that day, God decided to demonstrate naturally what He was accomplishing spiritually. There are no coincidences with God.

> We must return to God's moral code written on
> the hearts of all humankind.

Barbara shared that with God, affirming her dream via the webcast and the arch photo, she prayed nothing would hinder God's plans for our nation, especially His plans of restoration in Washington, DC. She prayed that our nation would walk into that preordained place of holiness and righteousness. Into a place of cleansing and purity.

Barbara said, "This nation needs a cleansing. It needs healing, not just physical healing, but from all the scars of past sins, from the Native Americans to the Black-and-white issues. There is a cry in the land. God is answering the prayers of the present intercessors and our ancestors and founding fathers, who laid the foundational stones for this nation."

Additionally, Amy Sabat shared that she had been praying concerning this vision. She believed that the Holy Spirit guided her to understand that part of the healing Barbara mentioned was the healing of the abortion issue in our nation, especially following the overturning of *Roe v. Wade*, which occurred seven weeks later, on June 22, 2022. That was a direct answer to prayer.

In Barbara's dream, everyone was healed, no matter the illness. God is restoring our nation. This implies that God will heal everything that needs to be healed in the United States of America. However, the enemy who seeks to steal, kill, and destroy will not go quietly. He will attempt to resist and impede God's plan for our nation. We must stay the course, keep praying, have faith, and expect God to move while we consistently take more and more ground for biblical values and healing in our nation.

We must keep our eyes open to what is happening in our nation and endeavor to remain fully focused on God's agenda and plan for our land. We must not only pray but also take time to listen for His divine instructions. When the word God gave me about the wellspring collided with the vision He had given Barbara, it ignited the faith of all involved and everyone with whom we shared the revelation. As in the book of Habakkuk, the vision is now plain.

SEVEN

THE TRUE NATURE OF HUMANITY

The foundations of a trustworthy government that our founders laid sometimes seem lost today in our nation. Moral corruption and division plague our country. Yet, there's a straightforward truth explaining everything we see—one critical truth that makes or breaks every good government. It is found in Romans 3:23: *"For all have sinned and fall short of the glory of God."*

This truth from the Word of God is not taught in any political science course. It was at the forefront of our founding fathers' minds as they drew the blueprints for our government when they prayed on that day in June 1787. Understanding this idea will have dramatic and drastic effects. What is that idea? It is the nature of humanity.

Is humankind inherently good or inherently flawed? What you conclude concerning human nature will have an outsized impact on how you believe government should be structured and which policies you will support.

If you believe in the goodness of humanity, you are constantly hoping for society to progress. You will look at everything wrong with your nation and the world and conclude that society has not reached its highest state. You will believe that the pinnacle of society will be achieved through human growth.

Society can only be improved through God's grace and the transformative work of the Holy Spirit. A nation will continue to struggle if it relies on intellectualism, education, and physical resources. The false notion of the necessity of government programs to achieve the common good accounts for trillions of dollars in government spending each year. Yet crime rates continue to rise, educational achievements continue to deteriorate, drug addiction incidences continue to increase, and so forth.

While these programs are not successfully reforming people and society, they empower cultural evolution. Societal leaders enforce their views through legislation, causing an increasing reliance upon the state because this is the sure way to make progress. If humanity is perfectible, then societal problems only require external solutions. These solutions, such as new programs and opportunities, guarantee positive outcomes. The faulty belief is that the answer to societies' problems lies within systems.

President Franklin Roosevelt called President Theodore Roosevelt the first great Republican Progressive. FDR, however, created modern progressivism. Responding to the rapid and staggering changes caused by the Industrial Revolution, the First World War, the rise of the titans of industry, and the Great Depression, FDR wanted to re-imagine the role of government.

> "The Declaration of Independence discusses the problem of Government in terms of a contract. Government is a relation

of give and take, a contract, perforce, if we would follow the thinking out of which it grew. Under such a contract rulers were accorded power, and the people consented to that power on consideration that they be accorded certain rights. *The task of statesmanship has always been the re-definition of these rights in terms of a changing and growing social order.* New conditions impose new requirements upon Government and those who conduct Government.[1]

Facing the disastrous impact of the Depression on individuals, FDR believed it was the role of government to act decisively:

Faith in America, faith in our tradition of personal responsibility, faith in our institutions, faith in ourselves demand that we recognize the new terms of the old social contract. We shall fulfill them, as we fulfilled the obligation of the apparent Utopia which Jefferson imagined for us in 1776, and which Jefferson, Roosevelt and Wilson sought to bring to realization. We must do so, lest a rising tide of misery, engendered by our common failure, engulf us all.[2]

So, FDR used the government to create and fund programs to put people to work and lessen a "rising tide of misery." These actions became entrenched in America's government and psyche. The government became the answer to all of society's problems. The national emergency created the opportunity for ideas and plans that, if unchecked and uncorrected, could destroy the foundations of the Republic.

God created government as just one of three institutions to care for us. God designed the family, the church, and the government to care

---

1. Franklin D. Roosevelt, Campaign Address on Progressive Government at the Commonwealth Club in San Francisco, California Online by Gerhard Peters and John T. Woolley, The American Presidency Project https://www.presidency.ucsb.edu/node/289312.
2. Ibid.

for the people He creates. Each has distinct responsibilities that are described in Scripture.

However, God's design has been twisted. The government has taken over, ignoring the role of the other institutions God created (family and church). Government has become the only solution, ironically accumulating power among a few people.

According to the Word of God, good government aligns and restores created order. (See Romans 13:1.) A good government realizes that truth cannot be redefined and that the change our world needs must happen in the heart and soul of each person.

Here's one example of how this plays out. In 2016, Justice Anthony Kennedy wrote the Obergefell same-sex marriage decision for the United States Supreme Court. This ruling created a constitutional right to same-sex marriage. Decades of substantial cultural and political developments have led to increasing societal acceptance of homosexuality. However, at the time of the ruling, most states seemed to lean toward preserving traditional marriage. Justice Kennedy used the word "evolve" in the decision. He described how the nation's morality had evolved, requiring a new interpretation of the Constitution. Thus, with one decision of nine men and women, everyone had to accept and provide for same-sex marriage.

Belief in humanity's goodness will lead to a constantly growing list of external solutions to our problems. Programs, government intervention, federal grants, and so on are viewed as the hope for humanity.

If you believe in the depravity of humankind, you prepare for the actions arising from man's sinful, selfish nature. You understand that unchecked power will create tyrants, a military without limitations will develop maniacal dictators, and welfare can easily create a nation of complacent people. Those programs designed to assist our fellow men are needed for a short period, not to become a lifestyle. If you believe in the depravity of humankind, you do not first search for external solutions to society's problems; instead, you seek internal solutions that change the hearts of men and women. Continually seeking God's guidance will strengthen the moral fiber of our nation.

It's no coincidence that the very First Amendment to the Constitution addresses freedom of religion. Our nation's hope must be in heart change, not external change. James Madison said, "If men were angels, no government would be necessary."[3] James Madison understood the depravity of man. So did Benjamin Rush, who wrote, "The gospel of Jesus Christ prescribes the wisest rules for just conduct in every life situation… Nothing but His blood will wash away my sins."[4] Our founding fathers, who grew up during the First Great Awakening, had a biblical worldview as well as an understanding of the weakness of humanity.

Leaders who understand the sinful nature of man will produce governments where religious freedoms allow the church the opportunity to flourish. A God-fearing nation is a necessity. A society that believes in the goodness of humankind will create a never-ending list of external solutions. They will always demand an increasing role of government in our lives. A society that knows humanity is flawed will look to *internal* heart solutions, positioning freedom of religion as the only hope to develop the morals of society.

Conservatives typically believe that morals do not evolve. They focus on known ideals and realize that government needs to be limited. At the other end of the political spectrum are the progressives, who believe morals are ever-changing.

---

3. "Federalist 51," Bill of Rights Institute, accessed February 13, 2025, https://billofrightsinstitute.org/primary-sources/federalist-no-51.
4. Benjamin Rush, *The Autobiography of Benjamin Rush*, ed. George W. Corner (Princeton University Press, 1948), 165–6.

> *Regardless of your political ideologies or affiliations, conservatives and progressives must seek redemption through Jesus Christ and receive a new nature (see 2 Corinthians 5:17) to impact generations.*

By understanding the true nature of humanity, we can continue to uphold biblical truths and seek to influence our communities, states, and nations. This is the part we have to play as citizens of the nation where we live, where God placed us (see Acts 17:25–27). The next step is understanding God's heart for nations.

The most critical factor in creating a good government is a correct understanding of the nature of humanity. If man is good, we can expect equitable outcomes given the right circumstances. External solutions are the only thing needed. However, both Scripture and experience tell us that humanity is flawed. Internal solutions are what is required. This is where the church comes in.

EIGHT

KNOWING YOUR AUTHORITY

Seasoned intercessors and prayer warriors must know who they are in Christ and understand the authority they have been given through the cross of Jesus Christ to be effective. This understanding is crucial in our spiritual warfare, a battle not against flesh and blood but against the spiritual forces of evil in the heavenly realms. (See Ephesians 6:12.) Without that knowledge, we could never effectively possess the enemy's gates.

Jesus says, "*Behold! I have given you authority and power to trample upon serpents and scorpions, and [physical and mental strength and ability] over all the power that the enemy [possesses]; and nothing shall in any way harm you*" (Luke 10:19 AMPC).

The authority Jesus is talking about is not in our physical strength. It is not brute force. It is a delegated authority. We can liken it to the authority of a police officer. When a police officer steps out in front of traffic to stop a vehicle, he cannot possibly prevent it with his physical strength. No, what stops the car is the authority delegated to him. The laws of the land fully back him.

It is the same with us. We cannot stop the forces of darkness in our own strength. However, we can stop the enemy with the delegated authority given to us through Christ. Just as the law backs a policeman's authority, our authority is backed by God Himself. We are backed by the power of an almighty God, who cannot be defeated. Ephesians 6:10 says, *"Finally, my brethren, be strong in the Lord and in the power of His might."* We walk in His divine power.

According to 1 Corinthians 12:27, we are the body of Christ. Jesus is the head; we are the body. If the power of God is in the head, that same power is also entirely in the body. Ephesians 2 tells us that when Jesus rose from the dead, He transferred His authority to us: *"But God…raised us up together, and made us sit together in the heavenly places in Christ Jesus"* (Ephesians 2:4, 6). We are seated in a position of power, in heavenly places in Christ Jesus, far above all the enemy's power.

Still, there is more: the Father put everything under the authority of Jesus, and then Jesus delegated it to the church: *"He put all things under His feet, and gave Him to be head over all things to the church, which is His body, the fullness of Him who fills all in all"* (Ephesians 1:22–23). To intercede with the authority Jesus speaks of, you must be fully persuaded that this authority is working in you. Jesus came to earth for one reason—to take back the authority Satan had stolen through Adam's disobedience. After taking back this authority, He freely gave it to those who would believe in Jesus and in what His Word says. (See Matthew 17:20; Mark 11:24.) One of the most powerful verses to increase our faith is these words of Jesus: *"If you can believe,* **all things are possible** *to him who believes"* (Mark 9:23).

Once you are convinced that God's power and authority are working in you, the next step is to saturate yourself in the Word of God.

> *When we enter our prayer room or times of intercession,*
> *the Word of God is the firm foundation on which we stand immovable.*
> *It is a powerful force.*

- The Word of God lights our path. (See Psalm 119:105.)
- The Word of God stands forever. (See Isaiah 40:8.)
- The Word of God proves true. (See Psalm 18:30.)
- The Word of God is pure and a shield to all who trust in God. (See Proverbs 30:5.)
- The Word of God is living and powerful. (See Hebrews 4:12.)

Nothing is more powerful than the Word of the living God.

Jesus spoke simple words that healed, calmed storms, delivered people from demons, and raised the dead. He knew His words carried power. Today, if we walk with Jesus, we have that same authority—His Word still has that same power. When we take His Word into our prayer time and into our times of intercession, nothing will be impossible, for His Word always accomplishes what it is sent for. (See Isaiah 55:11.)

Knowing and declaring the Word of God over your situation and nation will play a vital part in overcoming darkness and possessing the enemy's gates. What do you do once you know your authority and what the Word of God says? You exercise it or put it into action.

Ephesians 5:1 tells us to imitate God. How did God accomplish creating the earth? He spoke it into existence. Throughout the first chapter of Genesis, we see where God said, *"Let there be…"* and there was. Whatever He spoke came into existence.

Therefore, to imitate God, we must follow His example and call things that are not as they were. (See Romans 4:17.) We do that with the Word of God. The Word of God is God's will for our family, city, and nation. We must dig through the Bible, find the Scripture that applies to our situation, and begin to declare it—start calling those things that are not as they are.

"Death and life are in the power of the tongue" (Proverbs 18:21). If we speak negative words over our children, our spouse, or our nation, we are releasing death over those things. However, when we speak life over our children, spouse, and country, we release life into them and the situation. Perhaps what you see doesn't line up with the Word of God. That is irrelevant. Abraham's life didn't appear to line up with what God had promised him. Yet everything came to pass just as God said it would.

Joseph's life certainly didn't look like he would see his God-given dreams come to pass, but they did—just as God promised. It doesn't matter what it looks like or how we feel about it. What matters is what the Word of God says about it and what we do with that Word. The Bible says God's Word will not return void (see Isaiah 55:11); however, if we don't put it into action, we will never see it come to pass.

Think of it this way. The electric company supplies power directly to your house. However, unless you activate that power by flipping a light switch or turning on your furnace or air conditioning, you will never experience the electricity already provided. In the same way, you have been given authority and power through the Word of God, but unless you use it or activate it by speaking it out of your mouth, you will never see the fulfillment of those words. God's power is in His Word. Hebrews 1:3 says He is upholding all things by the word of His power. We must do the same thing. We must know our authority. We must saturate ourselves in the Word of God. Then, we must release God's Word into the earth, thereby possessing the enemy's gates. That is when we will see the fulfillment of His Word come to pass in our lives and our nation.

NINE

THE NECESSITY OF RESILIENCE

Possessing the gates of our enemy will not be a quick victory; therefore, resilience and tenacity must be part of the armor of the praying person. Resilience is the ability to recover from challenges, disasters, or change.[5] It is the ability to cope and arise from setbacks. The book of Micah captures the attitude of a resilient heart in this verse: *"Do not rejoice over me, my enemy; when I fall, I will arise; when I sit in darkness, the* LORD *will be a light to me"* (Micah 7:8).

Intercessors need resilience. Resilient believers endure. It's not that they face fewer challenges or trials; it's usually quite the opposite. It is not that they hide their head in the sand and refuse to see what is happening. No, the truth is that their hope is firmly planted in God. They keep their eyes on Him and can rise again, regardless of any attempts to knock them down.

---

5. *Merriam-Webster.com Dictionary*, s.v. "resilience," accessed January 26, 2025, https://www.merriam-webster.com/dictionary/resilience.

"When I sit in darkness, the LORD will be a light to me." When we look around our nation today, we see darkness growing, yet the light of God has not diminished. It still shines brightly. The resilient ones realize this and continue to walk in faith and hope, regardless of what they see, hear, and know to be facts. Instead of falling into despair, they face life, the challenges of family, and our nation head-on, knowing in whom they believe.

Is it easy to be resilient? No. *"Hope deferred makes the heart sick, but when the desire comes, it is a tree of life"* (Proverbs 13:12). In the past few years, our nation has endured many instances of deferred hope. I love how *The Message* Bible paraphrases this verse: *"Unrelenting disappointment leaves you heartsick, but a sudden good break can turn life around"* (MSG).

"Unrelenting disappointment." That means one disappointment after the other. It speaks of attacks and challenges that seem to be never-ending. I have witnessed more people praying for our nation in the past few years than ever before. Even with all that prayer, we have faced numerous disappointments. If we focus on the disappointments, we will become heartsick. We will become a people without hope. We will begin to see everything through the lens of disappointment. However, because our hope is firmly established in God and His Word, we can remain a people of hope.

How can we stay hopeful despite everything happening in our nation? How do we develop resilience? How do we obtain an unwavering faith in God and His Word, even when adversity comes? Cultivating resilience will give us the stability and faith to stand firm until we see God's perfect will fulfilled for our family and nation. Here's how we do it.

DEVELOP A FIRM FOUNDATION

A strong foundation in God and His Word is vital. We must know what the Word of God says about God's promises for us, our family, and our country. We can't just read the Bible and throw around confessions. We must be fully persuaded, just as Abraham was, of what God has said, whether it concerns us personally or our nation. Abraham *"did not waver at the promise of God through unbelief, but was strengthened in faith, giving glory to God, and being fully convinced that what He had promised He was also able to perform"* (Romans 4:20–21).

Abraham did not waver even though he was too old to have a child. Even though it seemed impossible, he refused unbelief. He strengthened himself in faith. How? By giving glory to God. He was convinced without question that God would do what He said He would do. Are you fully persuaded that God will fulfill His promises for your family? For your nation? If not, build a resilient faith by meditating on God's Word and giving glory to God for those precious promises.

Consistent Bible reading and study will deepen our understanding of God and His faithfulness. It will also solidify our foundation. It is the firm footing on which we stand. Set aside time each day to read and meditate on God's Word. As you do, you will find your faith in God becoming more and more resilient.

DEVELOP A STRONG PRAYER LIFE

> *Prayer is a necessity in the life of a believer and an intercessor. It is our lifeline, connecting us directly to God.*

Before we can have resilient faith, our prayer life must be established. Prayer is not complicated. It is simply a conversation with God.

Talking to God is a great place to begin. Then, add listening. If one person does all the talking, it's not a conversation; it's a monologue. In earlier chapters, I emphasized the importance of listening to God and asking Him how He sees the circumstances in our lives, nation, and world.

Prayer and intercession are the keys to staying encouraged. We pray to God to release the burdens of everyday life. We intercede to sense His perspective on matters. The emotional release of prayer and the direction we receive through intercession allow us to build resilience.

Prayer keeps our focus on God: *"You will keep him in perfect peace, whose mind is stayed on You, because he trusts in You"* (Isaiah 26:3). Consistent, daily prayer keeps our mind on God and our trust and hope firmly planted in Him.

> *Be anxious for nothing, but in everything by prayer and supplication, with thanksgiving, let your requests be made known to God; and the peace of God, which surpasses all understanding, will guard your hearts and minds through Christ Jesus.* (Philippians 4:6–7)

A prayerless life will be an anxious life. As we cultivate a life of prayer, God's peace becomes ours. This peace will surround us, going far beyond our natural understanding. His peace guards our hearts and our minds through Jesus. If our hearts and minds trust God, we will be resilient, knowing God is on our side and will fulfill His promises.

DEVELOP A SUPPORTIVE PRAYER GROUP

Community plays an essential part in developing resilient faith. "Two are better than one, because they have a good reward for their labor. For if they fall, one will lift up his companion. But woe to him who is alone when he falls, for he has no one to help him up" (Ecclesiastes 4:9–10).

Surrounding ourselves with other believers provides us with strength and encouragement. In the book of Acts, the early church consistently gathered to pray, teach, fellowship, and break bread, which helped them remain resilient in their faith.

> *Then those who gladly received his word were baptized; and that day about three thousand souls were added to them. And they continued steadfastly in the apostles' doctrine and fellowship, in the breaking of bread, and in prayers.* (Acts 2:41–42)

If you aren't already part of one, consider joining or forming a faith-based prayer group where you can grow together in God. Bonds are formed in such groups, which can be a great source of strength and comfort.

DEVELOP GROWTH AND STRENGTH THROUGH ADVERSITY

Adversity does not have to be destructive. It can be an opportunity to grow and strengthen our faith. James 1 teaches us this valuable lesson:

> *Consider it wholly joyful, my brethren, whenever you are enveloped in or encounter trials of any sort or fall into various temptations. Be assured and understand that the trial and proving of your faith bring out endurance and steadfastness and patience. But let endurance and steadfastness have full play and do a thorough work, so that you may be [people] perfectly and fully developed [with no defects], lacking in nothing.* (James 1:2–4 AMPC)

When you encounter a challenging situation, seek God's face. Ask Him to show you what you can learn. Ask the Holy Spirit to teach you to grow through it. Allow God to strengthen you through it.

> *Fear not [there is nothing to fear], for I am with you; do not look around you in terror and be dismayed, for I am your God. I will*

strengthen and harden you to difficulties, yes, I will help you; yes, I will hold you up and retain you with My [victorious] right hand of rightness and justice. (Isaiah 41:10 AMPC)

DEVELOP A RESILIENT TRUST IN GOD

Trusting God, His Word, and His timing is essential for resilient faith. This firm, immovable trust must apply when things are going well and also, especially, when circumstances seem uncertain. We can learn from Proverbs: *"Trust in the LORD with all your heart, and lean not on your own understanding; in all your ways acknowledge Him, and He shall direct your paths"* (Proverbs 3:5–6).

We cannot lean on our own understanding. Abraham trusted God even when asked to sacrifice his son Isaac. (See Genesis 22:1–19.) He trusted God to keep and fulfill His covenant promises even when circumstances seemed impossible.

It is not always easy to understand with our natural senses why we are going through adversity. Yet we must trust that God has a good plan for us. We can trust Him to bring His promises to pass at the appointed time. *"For I know the thoughts that I think toward you, says the LORD, thoughts of peace and not of evil, to give you a future and a hope"* (Jeremiah 29:11).

Resilient faith means trusting God, His timing, and His divine plan, particularly during times of instability and uncertainty. In those times, those seasons, we must stand firm in our faith without wavering, for then we will develop an immovable resilience.

In the following section of this book, we will encounter resilient individuals who have served as national gatekeepers. Although they have possessed the gates in various ways, they all share resilience.

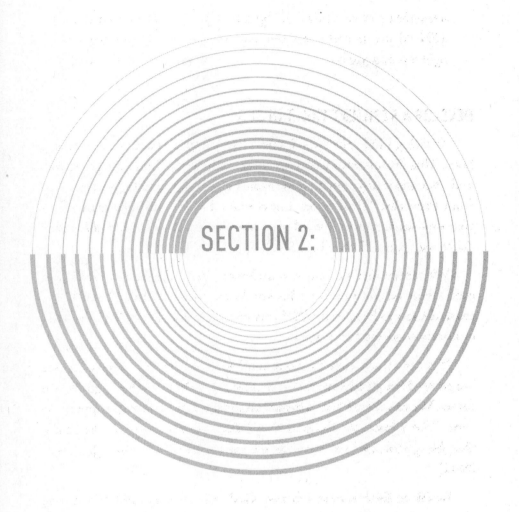

SECTION 2:

ORDINARY PEOPLE, EXTRAORDINARY CALLINGS

TEN

VICTORY AT THE GATE

"Mr. Gorbachev, tear down this wall."[6] President Ronald Reagan's powerful words delivered on June 12, 1987, marked a pivotal historical moment. This iconic line resonated with the global call for freedom, making it one of the most profound moments in modern history.

As President Reagan stood in front of the world, he declared a policy of freedom. He called upon Mikhail Gorbachev, the General Secretary of the Communist Party of the Soviet Union, imploring him to tear down the Berlin Wall that had split West Berlin for more than two decades. Under Communism, this wall controlled the lives of two million people.

---

6. "Remarks on East-West Relations at the Brandenburg Gate in West Berlin June 12, 1987," *The Public Papers of President Ronald W. Reagan*, Ronald Reagan Presidential Library, https://www.reaganlibrary.gov/archives/speech/remarks-east-west-relations-brandenburg-gate-west-berlin (accessed January 26, 2025).

Strategically positioned, President Reagan spoke right in front of the Brandenburg Gate. For two hundred years, that gate had stood as a memorial to freedom fighters. In 1987, as part of the Berlin Wall, it also symbolized the division of the democratic West from the Communist East, freedom from occupation, and West Germany from East Germany.

Contrary to popular belief, the Berlin Wall did not fall immediately after President Reagan's speech. It took another two years for the wall to crumble. The question then arises: what factors led to the wall's eventual collapse? How did President Reagan's speech contribute to this outcome?

Let's rewind to 1982, five years before President Reagan's speech. The Soviet-dominated German Democratic Republic (GDR) ruled East Germany with an iron fist. Head of State Erich Honecker promised death or imprisonment to anyone who dared defy the GDR. Many lost their lives to this evil regime. Yet a small group of men were willing to risk opposition, but not in the way one might think.

In 1982, a group of pastors from Leipzig initiated a weekly prayer gathering in a remarkable display of courage. This "Prayers for Peace" meeting was a beacon of hope in a region under the GDR's control. Despite the risks, these pastors would light forty candles every Monday, symbolizing the Israelites' forty years in the wilderness, and fervently pray for peace in Germany.

Initially, the authorities ignored them, but as attendance grew to thousands of East Germans, the GDR could no longer look the other way. The Stasi, plainclothes agents of the state security service, began infiltrating the meetings and recording the names of those in attendance. The GDR agents tried to intimidate the leaders, once leaving Rev. Christian Führer out in the snow to die. Many adults who attended the meetings were fired from their jobs. However, this did not deter these faithful prayer warriors. Youths replaced adults at the meetings, since they had no jobs to lose. Amid constant persecution and no visible answer to prayers, they continued interceding in weekly gatherings through 1987, the year that President Reagan gave his historic speech. The prayer group continued to pray and intercede.

In October 1989, during their seventh year of Prayers for Peace and two years after President Reagan's speech, the leaders felt the Lord leading them to do something different that week as they convened. They planned a candlelit prayer walk. The GDR leadership learned about the plan, so they mobilized armed troops and sent tanks to line the street leading from the church to the center of the city.

As a united group, the intercessors left the protection of the church, knowing the risk. Divine courage rested upon each one as they filled the streets with prayer and light from their candles. They emerged from the church so committed to freedom that they were willing to accept any consequences that would inevitably come. Much to their surprise, they were joined by 100,000 fellow candle-carrying Germans who supported their march for freedom. Facing possible death, the peaceful intercessors marched directly in front of the armed GDR troops that lined the streets that day.

Never had Honecker allowed this kind of defiance. In times past, troops would have immediately shot and killed any demonstrators. The GDR soldiers had guns pointed at the demonstrators. Russian-made tanks were lined up behind each soldier, ready with loaded machine guns. Still, the peaceful protesters continued to increase in number as they marched on. The brave demonstrators began approaching the soldiers, offering them lighted candles. Miraculously, the soldiers began to lay down their weapons and accept the lighted candles, joining the protesters. Eventually, the tanks backed away and returned to base.

Fifteen-year-old Antje Bakalov, a native of Leipzig, was there that night. That night, she had attended a movie with her classmates. She recalled, "When we came out, the entire train station was full of soldiers who pointed guns at us. Somehow, I remember thinking they looked confused and unsure what to do. We were told not to dare attend the demonstration or be kicked out of school. It sounded more like a challenge than a threat to a bunch of teenagers, and many of us went. I wasn't a believer then, and my parents had always kept me from knowing too much out of fear I'd ask too many questions and get us in trouble. But that demonstration was an eye opener on so many levels, and even though I didn't know God, I remember feeling this awesome presence I couldn't describe or understand at the time."[7] An unexplainable, awesome *presence*. The disgraced GDR leaders said, "We were ready for anything except candles and prayer."[8]

Ronald Reagan experienced that presence years before he courageously challenged the Soviet Empire to open to freedom. In 1970, then-Governor Reagan was nearing the end of his first term in California. An informal meeting at his Sacramento residence included Nancy Reagan, Pat and Shirley Boone, and Herb Ellingwood, the governor's legal affairs director. Ellingwood made it his practice to pray over Governor Reagan's chair every morning before the workday. Looking back, we now know the importance of this simple yet unusual act. Imagine the prayers that were answered over decades of Reagan's public service. I wonder if Ellingwood knew he was praying for a man who would become president of the United States and be instrumental in providing leadership in the fall of the Iron Curtain.

George Otis Sr., a pioneering Christian broadcaster, was also present on that pivotal day. At the meeting's end, people began moving

---

7. David Kubal and Intercessors for America, "What Lessons Can We Learn 37 Years After Reagan's 'Tear Down This Wall' Speech?" *The Washington Times*, June 10, 2024, https://www.washingtontimes.com/news/2024/jun/10/37-years-after-reagans-tear-down-this-wall-berlin-/.
8. Kubal, "What Lessons Can We Learn…?"

toward the foyer when Pat Boone asked, "Governor, would you mind if we prayed a moment with you and Mrs. Reagan?"[9]

Those gathered formed a circle and joined hands, and Otis began praying out loud. Otis's account showed that his prayers initially felt uninspired and directionless. But then, he later said, "the Holy Spirit came upon me, and I knew it."[10]

Otis's hand that was holding the governor's hand began to tremble, causing Reagan's hand to tremble too, as the tone of the prayer changed. After a few words of affirmation in which he addressed the governor as "My son," Otis began to declare God's plan to Reagan: "If you walk uprightly before Me, you will reside at 1600 Pennsylvania Avenue."[11]

Reagan took this seriously, calling it the "Divine Plan," despite the mocking and cynicism of political friends and foes. Over ten years later, in January 1981, Reagan took up residence at 1600 Pennsylvania Avenue when he was elected the fortieth president of the United States. As president, he believed that he was called to war against the growing evil of atheistic Soviet Communism.

Just two months later, Reagan was shot by would-be assassin John Hinckley Jr. Millions prayed, and God spared his life. Reagan believed God had saved him for a greater purpose. In 1982, the same year the Prayers for Peace meetings began in Leipzig, Reagan announced: "Let us now begin…a crusade for freedom that will engage the faith and fortitude of the next generation. For the sake of peace and justice, let us move toward a world in which all people are at last free to determine their own destiny."[12] When Reagan challenged the Soviet leader at the

---

9. Keith Guinta, "Ronald Reagan and the D.P.," *The Stream*, August 31, 2024, https://stream.org/ronald-reagan-and-the-d-p/.
10. Guinta, "Ronald Reagan."
11. Guinta, "Ronald Reagan."
12. President Ronald Reagan Speech to Members of the British Parliament, June 8, 1982, The History Place, Great Speeches Collection, https://www.historyplace.com/speeches/reagan-parliament.htm (accessed 26 January 2025).

Brandenburg Gate in Berlin on June 12, 1987, he wasn't merely reading words from a page. He was fulfilling his divine purpose.

> *Prayer, not policy, tore down the Berlin Wall. Policy alone is limited in power. Policy needs prayer to succeed.*

Two years later, in 1989, divine destiny collided with years of committed intercession, culminating in the powerful demonstration that broke the power of Soviet Communism that day. Honecker's leadership could not continue. Within days, he resigned, and Soviet Premier Gorbachev began tearing down the Berlin Wall. Policy and historical speeches alone could not accomplish this task. It took fervent, committed intercession from faithful prayer warriors who refused to give up.

Over forty years ago, President Reagan stood before the Brandenburg Gate, declaring, "General Secretary Gorbachev, if you seek peace, if you seek prosperity for the Soviet Union and Eastern Europe, if you seek liberalization, come here to this gate! Mr. Gorbachev, open this gate! Mr. Gorbachev, tear down this wall!"[13]

Do you hear it differently now? An inspired world leader declared freedom to people under the evil policy of communism. At the same time, intercessors were battling on their knees for freedom. Together, they fulfilled their divine purposes and a divine plan.

Prayer, not policy, tore down the Berlin Wall. Policy alone is limited in power. *Policy needs prayer to succeed.*

---

13. "Remarks on East-West Relations at the Brandenburg Gate in West Berlin June 12, 1987," *The Public Papers of President Ronald W. Reagan*, Ronald Reagan Presidential Library, https://www.reaganlibrary.gov/archives/speech/remarks-east-west-relations-brandenburg-gate-west-berlin (accessed 26 January 2025).

A president or governor alone did not achieve this tremendous breakthrough. No, it took many ordinary people to fulfill this plan of God. It took the fifteen-year-old Antje Bakalov, George Otis Sr, who was a broadcaster, Shirley Boone, and Herb Ellingwood all praying and participating in the plan of God. And don't forget all those faithful intercessors and pastors who prayed weekly for years or the youth who worked in the place of their parents who lost their jobs due to their commitment to pray. All these people played a vital role in seeing the plan of God fulfilled in His timing. God uses ordinary people like you and me to make a difference and bring breakthroughs.

ELEVEN

THE MOST IMPORTANT DAY IN AMERICAN HISTORY

What was the most crucial day in the history of our nation? What is the most vital *conclusion* from that day? Independence Day, July 4, 1776, is the day most celebrated in our nation—the birthday of the United States. But June 26, 1787, might be the most pivotal day in our nation's history. Without the occurrences of that day, our Constitution would never have been born. Our founding fathers utilized tools that changed our nation's history and began to possess the gates of the enemy that day. We can still use these tools today to participate in God's divine purposes for us and our nation.

By June 1787, our founding fathers had accomplished much. They gathered the colonies together, fought and won a war, and declared independence. They wisely structured a government called the Continental Congress. Yet a permanent government to structure the long haul was needed. They gathered in Philadelphia, Pennsylvania, to put the structure in place and write a constitution to replace the Articles of Confederation.

It was not going well; it was divisive and beyond dismal. Rough drafts of the Constitution were written. Delegates lobbied vehemently for their positions to be upheld. They could not come to a resolution within the Constitution as to how states would represent themselves. It appeared to be an insurmountable obstacle. People were becoming angry as tension filled the air. Our nation was about to dissolve. The opportunity to live out God's destiny was faltering. Some delegates even walked out.

Imagine what it would take to get to the point where some delegates threatened military action against other delegates. Frustration and disappointment abounded. Those who had risked their lives and fortunes in hopes of forming a new nation were unsure their dream would ever come to pass. Failure would mean that everything they had fought for and put their life and wealth on the line for had been in vain. All because of this one moment of division. On June 26, 1787, all seemed lost.

Suddenly, Benjamin Franklin arose and asked to speak to the assembly. By then, he was an elder statesman, known to be the least spiritual of all the founding fathers. This well-respected man slowly walked to the front of the gathering and, with great purpose, stopped at the podium. With immense conviction and immovable resolve, he spoke. I'll paraphrase his comments in modern English. "At the beginning of the contest with Great Britain, when we were in sensible danger, we prayed daily in this room for divine protection. It is the least spiritual. Our prayers were heard. They were graciously answered. Have we now forgotten the powerful friend? Or do we imagine that we no longer need his assistance? I have lived a long time and the longer I live, the more convincing proof I see of this. God governs the affairs of man."[14]

The hall was silent; you could have heard a pin drop. No one dared speak. Yet, this riveting speech *demanded* a reaction. Consequently, a motion was immediately made to change how they began their daily meeting. They agreed to start each day of deliberations with prayer. There was also a motion to have a chaplain attend the meetings to lead this daily prayer. Additionally, there was a motion to set aside three days to take a break from meeting to fast and pray. As the meeting adjourned that day, each man went his way to enter a time of prayer and fasting.

While they were apart on Sunday, Reverend William Rogers delivered a sermon about trusting God to give the wisdom to create a free and vigorous government. The following week, they reconvened on July 4, 1787. Everything was different. The anger was gone. There were no more undercurrents of animosity. There were now agreeable conversations where ill feelings had once resided. There was a distinct sense of accomplishing a critical task.

> *Prayer triggers cooperation.*
> *Prayer releases divine solutions.*

They didn't realize this monumental truth then; they only knew something was different. This is the power of prayer to transform division into unity and discord into harmony. Delegates were caught off guard by the new spirit in the air. One of the delegates, Jonathan Dayton,

---

14. "Franklin's Appeal for Prayer at the Constitutional Convention," Wallbuilders, accessed February 13, 2025, https://wallbuilders.com/resource/franklins-appeal-for-prayer-at-the-constitutional-convention/.

wrote in his journal, "...every unfriendly feeling had been expelled; and a spirit of conciliation had been cultivated."[15]

A committee was then formed, creating the representative structure of the House and Senate that we enjoy today—the House of Representatives. This structure, known as the "Great Compromise," was a significant breakthrough. It balanced the interests of large and small states, ensuring fair representation for all. It was the final, most important piece of the puzzle for the Constitution. The Constitution's final draft was produced in about six weeks; after years of fighting, it finally went through the states and was ratified.

Today, we must ask the same questions Benjamin Franklin asked the Continental Congress. "Are we smart enough now to not need the assistance of the Almighty? Have we forgotten our powerful friend? Why would we not want to solicit the Supreme in the affairs of this nation? Why would we not want to petition for the power of Providence to act? Why would we not ask the eternal God for wisdom? And why would we not appeal for divine power to solve the issues of today?"

Just as on that pivotal day in June 1787, change for our nation must begin with prayer. The Bible compels us to *"pray without ceasing"* (1 Thessalonians 5:17). It reminds us that prayer makes great power available—dynamic in its working. (See James 5:16.) There is nothing more powerful than a group of people gathering to pray for the will of the Father concerning our nation.

> *Again I tell you, if two of you on earth agree (harmonize together, make a symphony together) about whatever [anything and everything] they may ask, it will come to pass and be done for them by My Father in heaven.* (Matthew 18:19 AMPC)

A symphony with musicians who are not in tune is a grating to the ears. It makes a screeching sound that no one can tolerate. However,

---

15. Wallbuilders, "Franklin's Appeal."

when those same instruments are tuned and play in perfect synchronization, the collective sound is beautiful. Why? Because of their agreement, which produces an entirely different sound. They are harmonizing together, as the *Amplified Bible, Classic Edition* portrays in this Scripture. That is what the prayer of agreement sounds like to God—a beautiful harmony. Prayer is a powerful force, and united prayer is even more so.

In Acts chapter 12, the church faced persecution. Can you imagine that? Is it not the same in our country today? James, the brother of John, had been killed. When King Herod saw that this pleased the Jews, he went after Peter, throwing him into prison. The Bible says in verse 5 that constant prayer was made for Peter. Peter was bound in chains, kept between two guards; there was no way of escaping his impending death. Yet, one night, an angel of the Lord entered the prison and told Peter to arise. His chains fell off, and he left the prison at that moment. While the angel of the Lord appeared to Peter and released him from chains and prison, the people's prayers *summoned* the angel. We see this repeatedly throughout the Bible—prayer altering circumstances.

Prayer is potent, and when we add fasting to our prayers, it is even more so. Fasting is to the Christian life what training is to an athlete. Just as there are different levels of physical discipline (e.g., proper diet and strategic exercise regimen) as the runner gets close to race day, so we must go beyond our usual limits to gain a deeper level of spiritual intimacy with God or to experience victory in a particular battleground area of life. In the athletic arena, faithful commitment to the training schedule may make the difference between winning and losing. Similarly, fasting is a spiritual discipline that precedes the rigors of a spiritual battle and may well decide its outcome. Fasting will unlock spiritual power in your life like no other discipline. It brings the flesh into subjection, provides a heightened spiritual sensitivity in praying, and facilitates hearing the inner voice of the Holy Spirit as He illuminates portions of God's Word.

> **Fasting is to the Christian life what training is to an athlete.**

Some may think legislative proclamations of prayer and fasting are things of the past. Yet Tennessee proclaimed July 2024, a month of prayer and fasting. The proclamation stated in part: "we recognize that God, as Creator and King of all Glory, has both the authority to judge and to bless nations or states.... We...seek God's Mercy upon our land and beseech Him to not withdraw His Hand of blessing from us.... We call upon all those who are physically able and spiritually inclined to do so to join in a thirty-day season of prayer and intermittent fasting as we begin a new fiscal year as a means of seeking God's blessing and humbling ourselves to receive His Grace and Mercy, transforming ourselves, our communities, our State, and our Nation."[16]

Are you shocked that an American state would pass such a proclamation in 2024? The background of the sponsor, Representative Monty Fritts, is about as surprising as the proclamation.

Fritts was born and raised in Tennessee. He finished high school, then joined the Army National Guard, and got a job at Y-12, the nation's premier facility "in the manufacture, processing, and storage of special materials vital to our national security."[17] As an hourly employee, he was a Union Steward, protecting worker rights. He moved up the ladder at Y-12 and was deployed to Iraq with the Army National Guard.

---

16. A Resolution to Seek God's Hand of Mercy Healing on Tennessee, H.J.R. 803, Tennessee General Assembly (2024) (enacted). https://www.capitol.tn.gov/Bills/113/Bill/HJR0803.pdf.
17. "History," About, Y-12, accessed February 14, 2025, https://www.y12.doe.gov/about/history.

Fritts never planned on entering politics. He had retired from both jobs and could have taken life easy. But he sensed a calling and was not happy with how his elected officials represented him at the time. He ran and won.

Serving in the Tennessee legislature opened Fritts's eyes: "I don't think I fully realized until I got into the General Assembly how many forces of people and groups are trying to strip your freedoms away from you: from lobbyists who have immoral ambitions, to sometimes even politicians who have no connection to God Himself, nor to the Constitution that they've sworn to uphold."[18]

As he served, he noticed that leaders in Tennessee seemed to be infringing on the rights of law-abiding citizens because of the criminal behavior of others. He thought that the other lawmakers were trying to offer legislative solutions for what are essentially spiritual problems. "I am convinced that we public servants are obligated by oath to legislate and budget righteously. But I am even more convinced that leaders who call themselves Christians are obligated to point toward God's expectations,"[19] he said.

Looking at his state with spiritual eyes, Fritts saw a contrast: "Our state is likely the best place in the world to live; we have forests full of timber; fields full of corn, cotton, and soy; and rivers flowing with water. Our cost of living is among the lowest, and our weather is moderate. Industry and citizens from other states are moving to Tennessee. Yet, we have many leading indicators suggesting God may be withdrawing His hand of blessing from our state."[20] Those indicators included violent crime in schools, human trafficking, drug addiction, fentanyl, drunk driving, 9,000 children in foster care in the state, and corruption in the federal government.

---

18. United States Representative Monty Fritts, "Speech for Intercessors for America Event," (September 12, 2024).
19. United States Representative Monty Fritts, "Speech."
20. United States Representative Monty Fritts, "Speech."

"I wrote this resolution because I fear God's judgment and see the need for repentance among God's people as the only avenue to receive His hand of blessing again. I am concerned that the Lord may not give us many more chances to turn to Him. Our resolution seeks to bring about the awareness and repentance of God Almighty's people."[21]

Men and women like Fritts are everywhere. He did not imagine that he would make history with a proclamation of monthlong prayer and fasting. He was a retired man who took the first step to run for local office, seeking to bring godly values to his state.

We need this in every state. There are men and women representing all of us at the state level who are choosing what happens in our state, regardless of what happens federally. They're stepping up to possess the gates in their sphere of influence. They are declaring what they will allow within their gates. The most important thing a nation can do is gather and pray. Prayer puts us in humble submission before God. Prayer and fasting together take it to an entirely different level. Our country would not be here without constant prayer and fasting on the part of God's people. Nor will it continue to thrive without these two powerful forces. This is a historical fact necessary for our nation's well-being and prosperity.

We can all submit to God through prayer and fasting. In doing so, we join together to see the fulfillment of the covenant of God to Abraham, to possess the gate of the enemy, to be a blessing to all nations, and to impact generations. This is the only foundation for ensuring a good government for us and our families. If we understand this pivotal principle, we can have a good government. We will never have such a government if we don't understand its importance. Prayer and fasting are absolute necessities in beginning to possess the gates of the enemy.

Yes, fasting and prayer are a necessity—as well as being diligent to participate in the collective effort that desires to see the will of God

---

21. United States Representative Monty Fritts, "Speech."

manifest on earth, just as we see from these stories. This fulfillment required a speech from Benjamin Franklin; a timely, anointed sermon by Reverand William Rogers; and a Tennessee Representative, Monty Fritts, to see the will of God come to pass. God and man must work together to bring forth the will of God and be a continual blessing to our communities.

TWELVE

PRAYER *AND* ACTION MAKE A DIFFERENCE

"**U**nless the Lord builds the house, the builders labor in vain. Unless the Lord watches over the city, the guards stand watch in vain" (Psalm 127:1 NIV). There may be no better verse than Psalm 127:1 to summarize the halting construction of the Capitol Visitor Center (CVC) between 2000 and 2008. Now neatly tucked underground in the heart of Washington, DC, the sprawling structure embedded below the Capitol's East Plaza boasts four words engraved in gold: "In God We Trust," a reminder that where frustration abounds, trust in God must abound more.

Whenever Congress builds something for itself, people bristle. The construction of the Cannon House Office Building in 1908 sparked controversy because the building featured running hot and cold water—a luxury. Fast-forward more than one century to the half-a-billion-dollar underground complex of the CVC, and one can imagine the criticism it drew for being over budget and behind schedule. As late as 2009, nine Committee on House Administration members witnessed the last of the many speed bumps on the long road to completion.

One of the first in that series was 9/11. A little over one year after the groundbreaking for the CVC began in 2000, four hijacked planes crashed into the World Trade Center Towers, the Pentagon, and a field in Shanksville, Pennsylvania, located twenty minutes by air from Washington, DC. In the aftermath of this terrorist attack, members of congressional oversight committees found themselves gazing at the Capitol construction, anxiously picturing another potential Ground Zero and strategizing about how to keep their corridors from filling with acrid smoke. No one had fully considered the ability of the underground Capitol complex to withstand bombs, and new plans took shape to put better safety systems in place. The construction site resembled a gigantic sinkhole—not just in appearance but also as a financial drain, despite being only three-quarters the size of the Capitol.

New wounds seemed to reopen old wounds. As architectural plans grew to accommodate the nation's unfolding concerns over terrorism, members of Congress and their staffers carried the heavy burden of having expanded the size of the original footprint by two-thirds. It was big, more than they'd bargained for. Starting with each ancient tree earmarked for transplanting on the Capitol Lawn, every stage of uprooting and excavation—including the discovery of an undocumented, century-old well—caused those first years to feel like open-heart surgery. Unlike working in the private sector, where size and space are a virtue, working on Capitol Hill means feeling the constant frown upon size and expansion. Add to this balancing act the omission of Emancipation Hall. By 2007, plans were still unfinished to name and arrange the space honoring the enslaved laborers who built the original Capitol structure. Behind the scenes, designers scrambled to figure out which load-bearing halls could support the weight of the nation's sculpted heroes. Some heavy statues still needed reshuffling.

These weren't the only complexities. Long past the deadline and somewhere amid the noise of hammers putting the finishing touches on trim work, several congressional and faith leaders pointed out that there was no visible reference to God anywhere. Former South Carolina Senator Jim DeMint commented, "The CVC's most prominent display [proclaimed] faith not in God, but in government."[22] Despite pressure from Senator DeMint, former Colorado Congresswoman Marilyn Musgrave, former Texas Congressman Louie Gohmert, former Virginia Congressman Randy Forbes, and others, the words "In God We Trust" and the Pledge of Allegiance remained strangely missing from the architectural design. The group questioned why the pledge and the national motto were not included alongside *E Pluribus Unum* on the visitor center's walls. This would turn out to be the culminating, half-a-billion-dollar question.

It was a question that troubled former Tennessee Congressman Zach Wamp. A conscientious Christian, Wamp sought out former California Congressman Dan Lungren, a devout Roman Catholic serving on the Committee of House Administration. Congressman Wamp urged Congressman Lungren to sponsor a bill requiring the Architect of the Capitol to see that the design preserved the nation's Judeo-Christian heritage. He hoped to mirror in the CVC what was long ago engraved over the rostrum in the House Chamber and over the south entrance of the Senate Chamber. In early 2008, Democrats oversaw the House, and Congressman Lungren was a pivotal influence as one of only three conservative minority members on the committee. Several discussions needed to occur with key congressional offices to summon collaboration. The measure could move to the House floor if Congressman Lungren won the Committee of House Administration. So, at the eleventh hour, Congressman Lungren turned to his staff director and said with a look of quiet determination, "Get it done."

---

22. Alex Koppelman, "DeMint protests Capitol Visitor Center's 'left-leaning' displays," *Salon*, December 5, 2008, https://www.salon.com/2008/12/05/demint_cvc/.

But God had already set the scene to prepare hearts for action.

Providentially, since 2005, Congressman Lungren and his chief of staff, Victor Arnold-Bik, had made it a habit to informally invite representatives and staffers from across the aisle out for coffee or lunch. The goal was to build relationships. "I really can't overemphasize how much there is tension on the House Administration Committee,"[23] Arnold-Bik said. "The committee is like the 'mayor' for the Capitol complex, overseeing 435 kingdoms for 435 representatives, dictating parking, payroll—warning people not to walk down halls with asbestos, or politely telling offices not to barbecue on the fifth floor of the Cannon Building so no one would burn the place down."[24] He was convinced that any fruitful discussion and understanding on the committee would stem from both sides getting to know one another in a less intense environment. At first, there was skepticism, and invitations were declined. Eventually, the persistent coffee invites became an accepted, regular rhythm of hospitality.

According to Arnold-Bik, placing "In God We Trust" in the CVC wasn't controversial in the sense that it would never happen; in fact, Congressman Lungren's office suspected it would. The question was whether Democrats would minimize the importance of the motto by having it relegated to a dark corner. Congressman Lungren's staff members worked alongside the committee's two other minority members, former Mississippi Congressman Gregg Harper and former Speaker of the House of Representatives Kevin McCarthy, to collect signatures and gather co-sponsors for what would later be known as H.Con.Res.131. Although the location had yet to be determined, supporters of the bill envisioned that the motto would be front and center.

---

23. Victor Arnold-Bik, interview by Nicole Arnold-Bik.
24. Arnold-Bik, interview.

> *But God had already set the scene to prepare hearts for action.*

Also in 2005, Congressman Forbes laid the groundwork by mobilizing other leaders on Capitol Hill to join him in praying weekly in Room 219, just off the House floor. Several Christian leaders had detected an "orchestrated, well-strategized attack on the faith" around the country. They had a strong sense that they needed to pray together proactively and consistently. Burned into Congressman Forbes's memory is the moment when House Majority Leader Tom DeLay was originally permitted to use Room 219 for what came to be called the Congressional Prayer Caucus. Congressman DeLay walked away from Congressman Forbes about halfway down the aisle, then turned and said, "This could change the country."

Congressman Forbes cited the finishing touches on the CVC as being among the first pieces of evidence that these congressional prayer gatherings had indeed changed the country: "All of a sudden, we realized that things were coming up on the Floor about faith, about prayer. Before, we had just been blown over by them because you could never get everybody organized to stop them. Now that we…had over 100 members in that prayer caucus, we were making big differences on stopping legislation or getting legislation that we'd never been able to do before."[25]

Congressman Forbes believed that the congressional prayer movement, which began in 2005, prepared the way for what happened with the CVC in 2008–2009. This last milestone, and a turning point in the Capitol's construction, became more remarkable through a large circle of committed, conservative Christians, some quietly working and praying behind the scenes, while others leveraged in more obvious ways.

---

25. Congressman Randy Forbes, interview by Nicole Arnold-Bik.

Perhaps it was especially remarkable because the path forward had been incredibly thorny, more often among Republican leaders than between parties, according to Congressman Forbes and Arnold-Bik. Yet, God was at work, stirring His people to accomplish His purpose. In some cases, God stirred them to wait and not act. Checks and balances were at play even in the body of Christ. This was evident when more outspoken, evangelical congressional leaders took a backseat and allowed others to become the mouthpiece. This was also the case when members of Congress asked WallBuilders, an organization dedicated to presenting America's moral, religious, and constitutional foundation, to monitor the content of the displays and exhibits in the CVC, providing some much-needed counsel. Later, when WallBuilders founder and President David Barton implied that he might raise the volume to his readers and listeners about CVC's liberal, secular bias, he was encouraged to postpone any plans to publicize his concerns. There was a sense that applying more pressure might hinder rather than help their cause. So, Barton graciously waited. Ironically, for everyone invested, this was a chance to trust God completely with "In God We Trust."

The week the measure gained momentum, Arnold-Bik's wife, Cindy, who knew all the roadblocks encountered since Congressman Lungren had said, "Get it done," was at home praying. The jaw-dropping answer came when Liz Birnbaum, majority staff director for the Committee on House Administration (working under Nancy Pelosi, former Speaker of the House of Representatives), and Jamie Fleet, staff director working under former Pennsylvania Congressman Bob Brady, reached out to Congressman Lungren's office and promised: "We will work with you." The two Democrats were ready to push the measure through the committee and committed to do whatever was needed to make that happen. "At that point, we were having honest discussions over lunch or coffee," said Arnold-Bik, "and the way they looked me in the eye, I felt like I could go to the bank. I could cash that check."[26]

---

26. Arnold-Bik, interview.

Sure enough, the measure did pass the committee. Next, the bill passed the Senate with some technical amendments. When it came back to the House to be voted on by unanimous consent, Congressman Forbes demanded that the measure remove *E Pluribus Unum* entirely. He insisted that the measure include displaying the Declaration of Independence and the Pledge of Allegiance in the CVC and engraving "In God We Trust" in stone so it would not be easy to remove. When he got pushback, he reminded the House leadership that it was no longer just him but also the whole prayer caucus standing on this. Alluding to conservatives praying across the nation, he added, "You will have to say on national TV why you don't want 'In God We Trust.'"

At last, the House leadership conceded, and the bill for the CVC passed at 10:15 p.m. on July 9, 2009. Congressman Harper considered it a special privilege to manage the bill from the House Floor as a freshman congressman in 2009. "It was 410–8—that's pretty amazing," Harper said. "I thought the prayer mattered, but they prayed *and* worked the issue. It was something that needed to be done." He credited Congresswoman Musgrave and others who had worked hard for this in the previous Congress.

Congressmen Lungren and Forbes immediately began anticipating a lawsuit to stop the measure. Separately and unbeknownst to each other, they encouraged the workers to install the motto as quickly as possible. The morning after the workers completed the engraving, they told Congressman Forbes they had worked through the night, not knowing how the court would rule. An electrical engineering consultant who worked closely with those overseeing the lighting of the words later cited his surprise at seeing the project move forward as quickly as it did.

It seems that whenever God does a great work in the history of the church, it's always through a "circle of friends." That same maxim might also be said about the prayer circle behind the push to place the nation's motto in the CVC. Leaders in Congress gave Congressman Forbes much of the credit for what happened. However, he credited praying Americans.

"We prayed for H.Con.Res.131," Congressman Forbes said. "There were people praying across the country. Sometimes, we don't realize the enormity of the people's prayers in their prayer closets and the elderly ladies praying on their porches. The fact that a handful of Congress was praying is no more important than the prayers of those people who had carried this prayer for years, culminating in this kind of thing.... I believe when prayers are offered, [those prayers] resonate. They don't just come and go away; they continue. I would walk through the Capitol many times and almost feel the prayers from decades before, and I wanted to make sure that we weren't taking God's presence away."[27]

> *It seems that whenever God does a great work in the history of the church, it's always through a "circle of friends."*

Thanks to the prayers of intercessors and the tireless efforts of a small group of lawmakers, along with the favor of God, "In God We Trust" is now permanently inscribed in stone at the CVC, the House Chamber, and the Senate Chamber. Prayer makes a difference, and when you pray in alignment with God's will, you impact the future. We are all part of a bigger plan, and it takes a collective effort to bring God's plan to fruition.

Another gatekeeper, driven by her passion for protecting the unborn, successfully made her way to the Supreme Court, as we will discover in the next chapter.

---

27. Congressman Forbes, interview.

THIRTEEN

PROTECTING THE VULNERABLE

One of the most important means of influence in a nation is the work of Christians obeying God's commands. Throughout the Old and New Testaments, we are commanded to care for the vulnerable, especially the widow and the orphan. Many passages in the Bible speak of protecting those who cannot protect themselves.

We find in Deuteronomy 27:19 a very strong warning: "*Cursed is the one who perverts the justice due the stranger, the fatherless, and widow.*" The New Testament reinforces this in the familiar passage from James 1:27: "*Pure and undefiled religion before God and the Father is this: to visit orphans and widows in their trouble, and to keep oneself unspotted from the world.*"

The 1973 *Roe v. Wade* ruling positioned the US as one of the most perilous locations globally for the unborn. This ruling sparked nationwide prayers and played a key role in the establishment of Intercessors for America (IFA). From its inception, IFA recognized that abortion contradicts God's law, prompting the group to pray for the overturning of the Supreme Court ruling.

Throughout my prayers for the abolition of abortion on demand in America, while leading a national prayer network against this grave injustice, I've consistently felt as though we were praying for a specific individual. I believed that *someone* would eventually have to initiate action to bring about the end of *Roe v. Wade*. For decades, as millions joined in prayer, we collectively hoped for a person to take decisive action. These weren't occasional prayers; they were daily commitments.

As we prayed for someone during life's highs and lows, God responded by orchestrating events, providing protection, and offering gentle guidance. God excels in these types of unexpected narratives.

In 1973, high school sophomore Becky Currie from Mississippi entered her first political campaign, inspired by a female lawyer to run for student government.

Years later, Becky was navigating nursing school when she discovered she was unexpectedly pregnant. Despite some urging her to terminate the pregnancy, she felt God moved her heart to safeguard the life of her unborn daughter. It's astounding to think how the prayers aimed at preserving lives after *Roe v. Wade* also contributed to this one precious life.

After completing nursing school, Becky started her career in labor and delivery, a field she remains passionate about today. Each time a baby is born, she sheds tears of joy and gratitude, embodying God's love for every new life.

> *As we prayed for someone during life's highs and lows, God responded by orchestrating events, providing protection, and offering gentle guidance. God excels in these types of unexpected narratives.*

As millions offered prayers for her, she encountered numerous challenges, yet she always felt God's presence guiding her, having grown up in the Baptist church. Regardless of her experiences, she maintained a deep connection with God.

In 2007, she began considering a run for state office. She prayed: "Lord, show me if I should run. If this is of You, let me know." Then, she went knocking on every door across three counties.

She felt that without a divine endorsement, her election would not materialize. As the president of IFA, I understand the significance of praying for those in office. From the start of this organization, we have sought godly leaders to win elections and excel in their roles. How frequently have we underestimated this perspective? I ponder how often our prayers have been fulfilled unnoticed, particularly regarding individuals like Becky, whose contributions have gone unacknowledged for years.

Becky won the election in 2007 and continues serving as a Mississippi House of Representatives member. During her time in office, she has supported numerous bills aimed at protecting life. She has consistently relied on God's guidance for direction.

In 2016, she introduced and advocated for the Gestational Age Act (GAA). This bill was born from a personal experience Becky faced as a labor and delivery nurse: she had assisted in delivering a baby at fifteen weeks who fought valiantly for its life. Inspired by that courageous baby,

Becky sought to establish a law prohibiting abortions after this gestational period.

Despite her involvement in numerous pro-life bills, Becky understood that this specific bill would reach the Supreme Court as a challenge to *Roe v. Wade*, and it did. Some might question how she knew this. Yet, for a woman attuned to the voice of the Lord since childhood, it was unsurprising. She felt deeply that this bill was exceptional, and her intuition was validated.

The law encountered opposition from pro-abortion providers in the state, a common occurrence with pro-life legislation. It ultimately progressed to the Supreme Court. In the time leading up to the oral arguments, the Supreme Court underwent significant changes. The progressive justices who aimed to preserve unrestricted access to abortion and uphold the constitutionally weak *Roe v. Wade* decision diminished in number. In their place, three new justices were appointed, all of whom were constitutional originalists aware of the issues surrounding *Roe v. Wade*.

The evening prior to the hearing, I had the wonderful opportunity to meet Becky, who was recognized by IFA at a prayer event. I felt quite anxious about this encounter. God's presence radiated from her as if I could sense the countless prayers offered on her behalf. I don't think anyone has received as many prayers as Becky has.

The rest is history. The hearing went well, though someone in the court leaked a draft decision to the press. Finally, on June 24, 2022, the legally and morally bankrupt *Roe v. Wade* decision was overturned by the Supreme Court's ruling in *Dobbs v. Jackson*.

> *As you pray, endeavor to be a conduit for protecting the vulnerable in your sphere of influence.*

The *Dobbs v. Jackson* ruling is often described as having overturned *Roe v. Wade*, but this view is incomplete. God also inspired the rise of Becky Currie, who played a crucial role in this movement, alongside hundreds of thousands of intercessors who prayed for her. In fact, I believe she is the most prayed-for individual in the last fifty years of our nation. God caused Becky, through many prayers on her behalf, to possess the gates of her enemy, and she continues to fight today.

Becky was a regular student working through nursing school while thousands prayed, "Somebody do something!" Becky was the person whom God chose to be that somebody that day. You could also be that person, going through your daily life, whom God chooses to propel into His divine destiny. Through prayer and fasting, we can keep our eyes and ears open to God's plan for our lives and nation.

You, too, can possess the gates of your enemy through diligent prayer, intercession, and action. As you pray, endeavor to be a conduit for protecting the vulnerable in your sphere of influence. Remember, prayer and action are often necessary to overcome the enemy.

In the Old Testament book of Haggai, we find a partnership of two men with equally important, complementary jobs to do regarding the rebuilding of the temple. Joshua, the high priest, was tasked with impacting the spiritual realm, while Zerubbabel was in charge of the more practical task of rebuilding the temple. Both were necessary to rebuild the temple. Both were needed to rebuild and possess the gates.

FOURTEEN

INTERCESSION FOR THOSE IN AUTHORITY

One of the ways we can honor God is to undergird those He has placed in authority. Unfortunately, respect and honor for authority are lacking in our society today. Still, as Christians, we need to continue to pray and intercede for those who hold positions of authority in our city, state, and nation.

> *Let every soul be subject to the governing authorities. For there is no authority except from God, and the authorities that exist are appointed by God.* (Romans 13:1)

In addition, praying for those in authority over us is not a suggestion but a command from God for our good. (See 1 Timothy 2:1–4.). We must pray for our leaders regardless of our political affiliation or opinion. We must pray that God will give them wisdom and discernment as He leads and guides them; that they will listen for the voice of God, hear Him clearly, and obey Him quickly; and that they will follow Jesus Christ in all they do.

This applies whether we are happy with what our leaders are doing or not. It applies at local, city, state, and national levels. In doing so, we obey the Word of God. We cannot ignore what God has said on this subject. As we obey His Word, we empower those in authority to flourish and succeed.

From the beginning of George H. W. Bush's presidency in January 1989, the community and leadership of IFA sensed the importance of earnest intercession for him, his wife, Barbara, his cabinet, and all White House personnel. At that time, there was no way of knowing why this would be vital.

In November 1990, a small group was gathered to seek the Lord and pray for northeast Ohio. One of the people praying was John Beckett, president of IFA at the time. That night, the Lord had a different agenda. The US military was mobilizing for Operation Desert Storm, amassing troops and armaments in the Middle East, and President Bush was very much on the hearts of praying people. The president had made several confusing and contradictory statements about American motives in the war, mishandled some tax-related announcements, and struggled to maintain the public's trust.

As they began to pray, the people gathered sensed that the president was in a spiritual fog. John said they saw dark, foreboding evil spirits engulfing the White House and the whole city of Washington, DC, with a distinct mission to confuse the president and his staff, and one news release after another bore testimony to their effectiveness.

The group pressed on in prayer, asking for God's help to know how to pray, certain that they were touching on a matter of strategic importance to the Lord and the nation. Well over an hour had passed when a mighty sense of God's presence and power descended on the group. The prayer took on a new level of boldness, spiritual harmony, and drama. The room virtually shook as those in attendance took spiritual authority over the satanic strongholds and proclaimed a freedom for President Bush that would enable him to think clearly and exercise godly leadership. They could "see" the fog start to lift and sensed that the Spirit of the Lord was reaching the president in a fresh way.

The results of that prayer, and, of course, the prayers of many others, were profound. Within weeks, the US launched a major offensive that produced one of the most stunning victories in military history. Operation Desert Storm was the Gulf War's combat phase and began on January 17, 1991, in response to the Iraqi invasion of Kuwait in August 1990. Iraq's president at the time, Saddam Hussein, refused to end the unlawful occupation, even after a substantial buildup of coalition forces in the area.

Under President Bush's leadership, the US military responded to calls for help from Arab nations such as Saudi Arabia and Egypt. After just forty-two days of strategic, relentless aerial and naval attacks, followed by a swift ground assault, President Bush declared a ceasefire on February 28, 1991. At that time, most of the Iraqi forces in Kuwait had either surrendered or fled. Their army had experienced heavy losses of upwards of ten thousand troops, whereas coalition forces sustained approximately three hundred. The Gulf War victory was considered extraordinary, as the Iraqi military was believed to be the fourth-largest in the world, possessing a strong air defense network and an arsenal of chemical and biological weapons.

> *The group pressed on in prayer, asking for God's help to know how to pray, certain that they were touching on a matter of strategic importance to the Lord and the nation.*

Throughout this period, President Bush displayed a level of leadership that he had neither demonstrated before nor would replicate afterward. During this time, his thoughts were clear, his statements sharp; he maintained strong command. Public approval for him reached an all-time high.

Following that quick and decisive victory, President Bush felt burdened to lead the country in an expression of thanksgiving; he called on Americans to set aside three days in April 1991 to give thanks to God. Part of the official presidential proclamation reads as follows:

> Asking Him to judge not our worthiness but our need and protection, and knowing that the Lord gives victory "not by might, nor by power," we prayed for a swift and decisive victory [and] for the safety of our troops. Clearly, the United States and our coalition partners have been blessed with both. We thank the Lord for His favor, and we are profoundly grateful for the relatively low number of allied casualties, a fact described by the commanding general as "miraculous."[28]

God not only guided and protected the United States during the war, but He also gave this nation a president who could point toward the power of prayer that he had found while in the place of prayer.

One year later, on April 21, 1992, fifteen evangelical leaders met with President Bush at the White House. John was again privileged to be among them, representing Intercessors for America.

John asked the president how he wanted them to pray for him, given his unique position and the intensity of the pressures he faced. Without hesitation, President Bush said, "What I pray for is strength to do this job, to do what's right, and to be fair in the process. And then the family."

---

28. "Proclamation 6257—For National Days of Thanksgiving, April 5–7, 1991," The American Presidency Project, UC Santa Barbara, accessed February 3, 2025, https://www.presidency.ucsb.edu/documents/proclamation-6257-for-national-days-thanksgiving-april-5-7-1991.

Noting that there was much he could say about the subject, he continued, "We're caught up in ugliness in our family right now; because of what has happened in the primaries, they're going after my son."

> *The work of an intercessor never stops, and it is vital for godly governing.*

Ever since President Bush had taken office, his family had been under a microscope. As the 1992 election neared, the pressure intensified, zeroing in on his son Neil Bush, who was previously involved in a $200 million federal lawsuit related to the collapse of the Silverado Banking, Savings and Loan Association. The charges of gross negligence and abuse brought against his son weighed heavily on the president, even causing him to question whether he should run for a second term. In later years, President Bush's eldest son, George W. Bush, recalled: "It killed him to see Neil singled out because he was the president's son."[29] President Bush's wife, Barbara, commented that her husband was consumed with worry and a guilty feeling; he had also developed an irregular heartbeat and was suffering from exhaustion.

They responded to President Bush's request by praying with him right there. The president was genuinely grateful for this prayer. In fact, following the meeting, he commented to John how much he appreciated being asked how they should pray for him. Once again, I see the relevance of Paul's instruction in his letter to Timothy: *"I exhort first of all that supplications, prayers, intercessions, and giving of thanks be made for all men, for kings and all who are in authority"* (1 Timothy 2:1–2).

---

29. Emily Schmall, "George W. Bush Says Dad Pondered Skipping 2nd Term," *NBC Chicago*, November 9, 2014, https://www.nbcchicago.com/news/national-international/george-w-bush-says-dad-pondered-skipping-2nd-term/1989474/.

President Bush ran for reelection in 1992 but was defeated by Bill Clinton. After the loss, Bush lamented that the nation never knew his "heartbeat." Additionally, he wondered if his presidency would become only an "asterisk" of history. However, time has shown that he is appreciated for his competency in foreign and domestic policy and his track record as a public servant who served as president and was a decorated war hero.

The work of an intercessor never stops, and it is vital for godly governing. President George H. W. Bush was a recipient of the mighty gift of intercession. On this side of heaven, we may never know what all the prayers offered up for this man accomplished. Nevertheless, we can have faith that God heard every one of those prayers, answering them according to His will.

James 2:20 says, *"Are you willing to be shown [proof], you foolish (unproductive, spiritually deficient) fellow, that faith apart from [good] works is inactive and ineffective and worthless?"* (AMPC). Faith and good works go together. While the job of an intercessor is never-ending, we must stay attuned to the Spirit of God concerning interceding for those in leadership. As these men and women purpose to guide our nation, we must diligently intercede for them. God will reveal to us exactly *how* to pray for them. Our prayers for those in authority demonstrate our part in possessing the gates, blessing the nations, and impacting generations.

FIFTEEN

BLESSING LEADERS BLESSES THE NATION

We can bless our nation by blessing those people who are in authority. There are many ways to do this: prayer, our words, and even writing letters of encouragement.

God expects us to use our words to build up, not tear down. Some of the things we hear Christians say about those in authority are vile words that should not be coming out of the mouth of someone who claims to follow Christ. Why? We are supposed to use our words for good. We are to keep our eyes on God and what He says about a person. Our job is to continue to try to see the best in others while loving them just as the Word of God commands. God loves them, even when they are not walking with Him. And love—God's love—never fails. (See 1 Corinthians 13:8.)

Matthew 12:34 says, *"Out of the abundance of the heart the mouth speaks."* If we meditate on God's Word and pray for His guidance, He will supply us with words of life and encouragement. However, if we meditate on what the news media is saying or the negativity and criticism of those in authority, the words that come out of our mouths may be harmful instead of helpful. *"For by your words you will be justified, and by your words you will be condemned"* (Matthew 12:37).

When we observe those in authority, let's do so with eyes of faith and love. Let's ask God to show us what He would have us declare over them and refuse to speak negatively about them.

Throughout the New Testament, we find the apostles writing letters to encourage the body of Christ. One such example is Paul's letter to the Philippians, in which we read:

> *I thank my God upon every remembrance of you, always in every prayer of mine making request for you all with joy, for your fellowship in the gospel from the first day until now, being confident of this very thing, that He who has begun a good work in you will complete it until the day of Jesus Christ.* (Philippians 1:3–6)

Not only did they write to encourage but also to pray and declare the Word of God over them.

> **God expects us to use our words to build up, not tear down.**

In this world of texting and messaging, it takes time and effort to sit down and write someone a note to encourage them. However, I know from experience that this kind of encouragement has far-reaching effects. What if you sat down and wrote one letter of encouragement a week to someone in authority in your city, state, or nation? It would require only a few moments of your time, but it could make a world of difference. We can only imagine the daily criticism our president, vice president, governors, and other leaders face. What if your letter released grace and an anointing over them to help them overcome obstacles and lead our nation with righteousness and truth? What if your letter, based on God's Word, brought a breakthrough they needed? What if your letter was still producing fruit for generations to come? What if your prayer-filled letter brought refreshment to the weary and heavy laden?

Tracy Bost, wife of Illinois Congressman Mike Bost, noticed that after President Trump was sworn into office in 2017, he was constantly bombarded with harsh criticism. The onslaught of negativity against the president in the media and Washington deeply disheartened Tracy. She wanted to make a difference.

Tracy invited friends and contacts in Illinois to write Bible verses for the president on index cards. She and her husband, Congressman Bost, expected to receive about thirty cards back but instead received hundreds. Tracy explained, "The cards didn't just have Scriptures on them. Some had heartfelt prayers [for] President Trump. On the cards from children, there were also drawings. I read each one before passing them on to my husband to deliver to the President."[30]

One of the cards came from a ninety-year-old woman. She wrote, "I have never written to a president, but I'm depending on you, and I pray into you every day that you'll straighten this country out—it needs it so bad."[31]

Congressman Bost delivered the prayer cards without knowing whether President Trump would see them. Months later, he attended a bill-signing ceremony in the Oval Office. When President Trump heard

---

30. Tracy Bost, interview by Nicole Arnold-Bik.
31. Abigail Robertson, "Letters Came in the 'Hundreds': The Prayer Notes the President Reads 'Every Day,'" *CBN*, March 7, 2018, https://cbn.com/news/us/letters-came-hundreds-prayer-notes-president-reads-every-day.

Congressman Bost's name, he immediately began wondering aloud how he knew the name. Bost said, "He all of the sudden turns at me and goes, 'Bost, Bost, prayer cards!'"[32] Vice President Mike Pence told Bost, "We read these every day and they're so wonderful."[33] That day, a photograph was taken of President Trump and Congressman Bost with the prayer cards. Unfortunately, when the picture was posted on social media several months later, it was used to falsely accuse both Trump and Bost of being "out of touch" about the school shooting in Parkland, Florida. This shows how obedience to the promptings of the Holy Spirit does not mean everything will be perfect. However, all of those prayers encouraged President Trump and his staff. The prayers hit the mark, which is what "intercession" literally means in the original language in the New Testament.

Knowing that the cards encouraged President Trump, IFA took up the charge, asking praying Christians in the network to submit prayer cards. Hundreds of thousands of cards were submitted from all over the world. I read many of these notes, and they were deeply touching—full of Bible verses and prayers.

Congressman Bost served for twenty years in the Illinois state legislature and was then elected to the US House of Representatives in 2015. As an elected official, Bost knew the importance and the impact of being prayed for. "Scripture is pretty clear that we need to pray for our leaders," Bost has said. "You know what? You never go wrong when you pray for somebody."[34]

> *Praying for our leaders, whether we like them or not, is essential to impacting generations.*

---

32. Robertson, "Letters Came."
33. Robertson, "Letters Came."
34. Robertson, "Letters Came."

Bost insists that it is vital to pray for our elected officials. The only intercession that is commanded in the New Testament is that done on behalf of governmental leaders: *"Therefore I exhort first of all that supplications, prayers, intercessions, and giving of thanks be made for all men, for kings and all who are in authority."* (1 Timothy 2:1–2).

Again, this command to intercede is not dependent on whether we agree with our elected officials or their party affiliation. Bost models this for us. He said, "I served with Barack Obama in the state of Illinois. Know him quite well. Don't agree with him—didn't agree with him on quite a few things—but I never [didn't pray] for him."[35]

Praying for our leaders, whether we like them or not, is essential to impacting generations. The Lord may give us ideas of how to act as we pray. May we be as bold as Tracy Bost in responding. Her simple act of encouragement made a huge impact. What impact can we make for our leaders? Pray and seek God for insight into the answer to this question. It will make a difference, just as it did for President Trump.

---

35. Robertson, "Letters Came."

SIXTEEN

STANDING FOR CHRIST, LOSING POPULARITY

God's promise to Abraham to possess the gates, bless the nations, and impact generations sounds like it would always be positive. Yet the Lord's followers throughout the ages have often been slandered, defamed, intimidated, and mistreated. It is vital to have thick skin to experience the fulfillment of this covenant.

There are many people I could tell you about whose stand for Christ has put a target on their backs, but I want to focus on a man and woman from Oklahoma.

RYAN WALTERS

Ryan Walters was a widely popular and admired history teacher in the small town of McAlester, Oklahoma. His advanced placement classes in US history, world history, and government showcased his love of teaching. He validated his students and encouraged interactive debates on key historical issues. In 2016, his peers nominated him as a finalist for Oklahoma Teacher of the Year.

During his teaching career, his students and fellow teachers couldn't tell and didn't care whether Walters was a Republican or a Democrat. They liked him and felt Walters and his family fit in very well with small-town life and an education system that functioned within their system of shared values.

A transformation occurred in 2019 when Governor-elect Kevin Stitt asked Walters to be part of an education working group that advised the incoming administration.

> *It is vital to have thick skin to experience the fulfillment of this covenant.*

Walters stepped into the cultural wars of education, using his new platform to promote godly ideas and values for education in Oklahoma. He began writing commentaries for conservative magazines and posting "car videos" where he expounded on the ills of the failing Oklahoma Public School system. The reaction to Walters's transformation was a display of vitriol-filled hatred accompanied by name-calling, hate messages, and unrelenting attacks in the media. Walters had opened up a spiritual dimension that displayed the battle for the hearts and minds of our nation.

In 2020, Walters was appointed Oklahoma's Secretary of Public Education. On January 9, 2023, Walters became Oklahoma State Superintendent of Public Instruction.

Since he took office on January 9, 2023, Ryan Walters, Oklahoma's Secretary of Public Education, has publicly named organizations and individuals promoting pro-LGBTQ agendas. Consequently, Walters found himself targeted.

Walters sought to impact generations during his first eighteen months in office. He publicized the academic failures in Oklahoma's largest school district, Tulsa Public Schools (TPS), where only 14 percent of the thirty-six thousand students read at grade level. Despite harsh criticism from some, a public outcry demanded the superintendent responsible resign.

Walters quickly responded to the Biden administration's proposed Title IX rules that created special rights and privileges for transgender students, saying, "I believe every student is created in God's own image. They're all precious individuals, and we need to be treating them that way. We're not going to allow left-wing indoctrination in the classroom; we're not going to allow any kind of gender ideology being pushed on kids."[36]

Walters upheld policies requiring students to use bathrooms consistent with their biological sex. Protesters accused him of murdering an Oklahoma transgender student who had a confrontation with classmates in a girls' bathroom and that night died by suicide. Then, more than 350 LBGTQ+ organizations, activists, and celebrities joined in and urged immediate action against Walters. Supporters of the LBGTQ+ community shouted, "You murdered Nex Benedict and his blood is on your hands."[37]

---

36. News 9, "'A Lot of Lies,' Ryan Walters Responds to Edmond Public Schools Challenge," *News 9*, February 27, 2024, https://www.news9.com/story/65de150fd581d7065533cf50/a-lot-of-lies-ryan-walters-responds-to-edmond-public-schools-challenge.

37. Gabe Woolley (@GabeGwoolley), "This is living documented proof that we have to continue raising the standard for education and our children in the state of Oklahoma. THIS behavior is the product of the broken family, indoctrination, and an entitled spirit. We are taking our children back, Oklahoma!" X, April 17, 2024, https://x.com/GabeGwoolley/status/1780793319548678264.

In February 2024, Walters objected to books in the Edmond Public Schools library that he deemed unsuitable for certain age groups. As a result, Edmond Public Schools filed a lawsuit against him. His response: "What you see here are districts that want no accountability. They want to go back to a time when pornography was on the shelves in our schools. They want books like *Gender Queer*, and *Flamer* made available to kids of all ages, and we're not going to stand for it, we have to have accountability."[38]

Walters spearheaded new state guidelines incorporating the Bible in the curriculum to emphasize the historical, literary, and secular benefits. It's not surprising that this effort was met with opposition and resistance. Walters was clear on the desired academic outcomes: "The Bible is an indispensable historical and cultural touchstone. Without a basic knowledge of it, Oklahoma students cannot contextualize our nation's foundation properly, which is why Oklahoma educational standards provide for its instruction. This is not merely an educational directive but a crucial step in ensuring our students grasp our country's core values and historical context."[39]

Sometimes, we can't identify the spiritual entities that seek to destroy our students—and, ultimately, our nation—until someone musters the strength to speak out in the public square. Walters did just that.

---

38. News 9, "'A Lot of Lies.'"
39. Oklahoma State Department of Education, "Walters Requires Bible Be Taught in Oklahoma Classrooms; Teaching Will Incorporate the Bible as an Instructional Support," Ryan Walters, State Superintendent of Public Instruction, Oklahoma State Department of Education, June 27, 2024, https://kfor.com/wp-content/uploads/sites/3/2024/06/Walters-Requires-Bible-be-Taught-in-Oklahoma-Classrooms20.pdf.

E'LENA ASHLEY

Another bold person from Oklahoma is E'Lena Ashley. Raised in California, Ashley moved to Oklahoma in 2006 to support her elderly mother. Uncertain of the future, she prioritized her mother's needs and chose to be by her side.[40]

Once Ashley settled in Tulsa, she volunteered in the Republican headquarters office, where she became aware that things were awry at the Tulsa Public Schools (TPS). She attended a school board meeting and listened as the board members debated who was responsible for the hundreds of thousands of dollars missing from one of the TPS accounts. Seeing little to no accountability, she knew something desperately needed to change.

When a school board seat became vacant in Ashley's district, she began praying for whoever would volunteer to run. When no one stepped forward at the last minute, Ashley decided to run. No one was more surprised than she was when she won in April 2022.

Ashley credited her win to God and the people who had gathered around her to pray and help her campaign. She came from outside the worlds of politics and education. She is a US Army veteran who served in military intelligence, worked for the Department of Veterans Affairs, and raised three children as a single mom. (The position on the school board proved to be one of the most challenging undertakings she had ever experienced.)[41]

Much of Ashley's campaign support originated with a unique group, the City Elders, founded by Jesse Leon Rodgers, a former missionary to Singapore who envisioned bringing together senior citizens committed to biblical reformation. Schooled in fundamental principles of faith, they get wisdom from their years of experience in various professions

---

40. "Board of Education," Tulsa Public Schools, accessed February 17, 2025, https://www.tulsaschools.org/about/board-of-education.
41. Nancy Huff, "The Prayer That Rocked the State," *Intercessors for America*, August 20, 2023, https://ifapray.org/blog/the-prayer-that-rocked-the-state/.

as pastors, church leaders, educators, doctors, lawyers, small business owners, and corporate management. Not ready to sit on the sidelines and let their country go downhill, they began meeting once a week to pray and plan on how to take spiritual authority over Tulsa.

Their goal is to determine the city's spiritual needs and take action to make the city a place where families flourish, and God is exalted. During Ashley's campaign, they talked to their neighbors, knocked on doors, passed out flyers, and planted yard signs. Once Ashley was elected, they continued to meet regularly with her to ensure she had the information, prayer, and support to succeed in her job.

As a school board member, Ashley immediately began questioning programs and budget proposals that seemed illogical to her. Before she approved any measure, she had to understand its impact on the children. With this bold approach, it didn't take long for her to uncover wrongdoing.

During one meeting, the superintendent presented the board with a copy of the nearly $700 million proposed budget for the upcoming school year. The expectation was that everyone would approve the budget proposal by the end of that meeting! The assumption was that no one ever read the budget, as it was much too complicated and lengthy, and there wasn't enough time to peruse it in detail.

Ashley thumbed through the stack of papers and alerted the board she would need more time to review the budget before approving it. The silence in the room was almost palpable as everyone looked at her in unbelief. She had no way of knowing then that her refusal to approve that budget would result in the uncovering of a significant embezzlement scheme of over $343,000 by a Tulsa school administrator. Ashley counted it as a win for God.

As events revealing corruption, mismanagement, and negligence unfolded, Ashley reminded everyone who would listen that "our children deserve better than failing schools." Her cry for better schools as justice for the children brought public attention to the steady decline of student test scores from 2015 to 2023. When the public realized those eight declining years coincided with the tenure of the current TPS superintendent, they brought intense public pressure for the TPS superintendent to resign. In only a matter of weeks, much to everyone's surprise, the superintendent abruptly resigned, allowing the Oklahoma State Superintendent of Education, Ryan Walters, to request the new interim superintendent to put together a comprehensive plan to increase reading, math, and science scores in Tulsa's public schools. It was another win for God.

Like Walters, Ashley was celebrated until she took a stand for Jesus. On May 20, 2023, she was asked to speak at the commencement services for East Central High School in Tulsa.

"Standing before the students and their families, Ashley unfolded the paper she thought contained her well-worded prayer of blessing. She looked down and realized she was holding the dry cleaner's receipt for cleaning her commencement robe. After the initial shock, she asked God for help: 'OK, Lord, it's just You and me; help me to remember my prayer of blessing I wrote for these children.'"[42] After taking a deep breath, she said: "I pray in the name of Jesus Christ that each one of you would walk forward from this moment in the excellence and love of God. That He would guide you, direct you, and draw you to your ultimate goal."[43] With that, she proceeded to deliver her prepared comments.

> The prayer lasted a mere 18 seconds, but that one mention of the *name of Jesus* set off a firestorm of adverse reactions far beyond reason, thrusting E'Lena into a vicious attack against her, personally.

---

42. Huff, "The Prayer That Rocked the State."
43. Burt Mummolo, "Tulsa Public Schools Board Member Criticized for Prayer at Graduation," *News Channel 8 Tulsa*, June 27, 2023, https://ktul.com/news/local/tps-board-member-criticized-for-prayer-at-graduation.

The local newspaper derided her with a barrage of negative articles. Social media trolls called her names and harassed her. The Tulsa public school superintendent and a fellow board member wrote open letters condemning her for violating the US Constitution and the TPS students' religious rights. In a matter of days, the threats of lawsuits began. The first threat came from the Wisconsin-based Freedom From Religion Foundation. The organization's website says it actively pursues cases it perceives to be violations of the First Amendment.[44]

Not long after Ashley's eighteen-second prayer, Oklahoma's then newly elected Oklahoma Superintendent of Public Education, Walters, and State Senator Dana Prieto showed up on the front lawn of the Tulsa Public Schools Administrative office building to present Ashley with more than 2,000 letters from Oklahomans who supported her commencement prayer. A contentious crowd greeted the state superintendent, waving banners, shouting obscenities, and physically pushing and shoving anyone who supported Superintendent Walters's efforts to show massive support for Ashley.

She saw some big, rough-looking guys who quieted the crowd and called out the troublemakers. Amazed that the crowd obeyed these men, Ashley thanked God for their presence. Later, she learned the "big guys" came from God's Shining Light, a church in the same TPS District 4 she represented. Pastor Dixie Pebworth sent some men in his Celebrate Recovery program to assist with crowd control. Pastor Pebworth, a staunch supporter of Ashley, gave his life to Jesus while incarcerated in an Oklahoma prison for selling illegal drugs. Miraculously, after being released early, he founded God's Shining Light church to minister to former inmates needing help transitioning back to life outside of prison bars.

---

44. Huff, "The Prayer That Rocked the State."

On the last Monday of every month, God's Shining Light opens its doors to anyone concerned about the schools in TPS District 4. Volunteers from the church serve dinner while Ashley answers questions and gives updates on what is happening in TPS and District 4 schools. Attendance easily rivals most parent-teacher organizations in any school.

> *They are ordinary people who say yes to God, and He strengthens them in the face of accusation.*

Ashley and Walters have been maligned and misunderstood by many. They are ordinary people who say yes to God, and He strengthens them in the face of accusation. They possess the gates of education in Oklahoma and bless the children and families in their districts and the state. But they don't do it alone. They are supported and uplifted by intercessors.

The vehement opposition to Ryan Walters and E'Lena Ashley may be difficult to understand. After all, Walters's positions were considered mainstream five years ago, and Ashley's short prayer would have been acceptable in her state just decades ago. What is fueling the fury? Demonic philosophies that are undermining the nation.

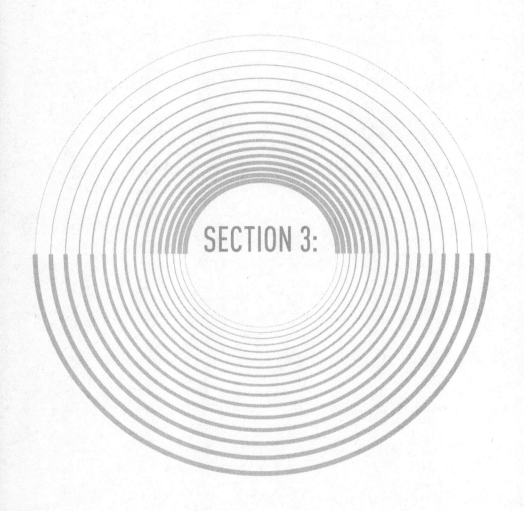

SECTION 3:

EXPLOITING SIN FOR CULTURAL CHANGE

SEVENTEEN

RETURN TO THE TOWER OF BABEL

"Return to the Tower of Babel"? What? Most people have never heard the positive message of this Bible account. Yet we can learn a profound lesson from this historic story. Humanity has always wanted to organize, centralize, and dominate to achieve more and more, just like when the people gathered to build a tower to the sky at Babel. This was the first time a one-world government was attempted. God put a stop to it. His divine protection brought it to a halt. (See Genesis 11:1–9.)

In Genesis 1:28, God told Adam to be fruitful, multiply, and fill the earth. This command still applies to us today. God's protection demands that we remain diverse in our countries and languages. Any attempt to consolidate power should be temporary, similar to how organizations like NATO or the UN operate. These entities may become unmanageable if we allow them to expand without limits. This serves as a cautionary tale reminiscent of the Tower of Babel.

We have to go back to the flood to understand the implications of what happened with the Tower of Babel. The biblical account of the flood presents this event as a godly global reset instituted because of the corruption and wickedness of the whole earth. The Bible says:

> *The LORD saw that the wickedness of man was great in the earth, and that every intent of the thoughts of his heart was only evil continually. And the LORD was sorry that He had made man on the earth, and He was grieved in His heart. So, the LORD said, "I will destroy man whom I have created from the face of the earth, both man and beast, creeping thing and birds of the air, for I am sorry that I have made them."* (Genesis 6:5–7)

Although God did judge the earth and its corruption, His judgment was balanced by His grace toward Noah and his family, whose lives were spared because Noah had faith and found favor with God. After the flood, Noah became a farmer and planted a vineyard. One night, he drank too much wine and became intoxicated. Unfortunately, his son Ham discovered his father in a compromising situation. Ham drew attention to Noah's mistake, telling his brothers, Shem and Japheth, about it.

> **The biblical account of the flood presents this event as a godly global reset instituted because of the corruption and wickedness of the whole earth.**

The brothers' response was to help their father cover his sin. They did not even look at their father; they went into the room with their backs toward their father and covered him completely. These were two very different actions. One brother uncovered sin, while the other brothers covered the sin. (See Genesis 9:18–29.) Today, we still see the consequences of these actions.

In Genesis 9:25–27, we read an intriguing section of Scripture: "Then he said: 'Cursed be Canaan; a servant of servants he shall be to his brethren.' And he said: 'Blessed be the LORD, the God of Shem, and may Canaan be his servant. May God enlarge Japheth, and may he dwell in the tents of Shem; and may Canaan be his servant.'" Because of Shem's leadership in covering his father's sin, Ham's descendants would serve Shem's descendants. The Bible teaches that the descendants of Japheth would live in Shem's tents, and Ham's descendants would be Shem's servants.

One specific son of Ham was Nimrod, who was known as a mighty warrior and leader. Though the Bible doesn't expressly state it, Nimrod may have been involved in the building of the Tower of Babel. Genesis 11 gives us the motive for the construction of the tower of Babel: "Now the whole earth had one language and one speech.... And they said, 'Come, let us build ourselves a city, and a tower whose top is in the heavens; let us make a name for ourselves, lest we be scattered abroad over the face of the whole earth'" (Genesis 11:1, 4).

This is the opposite of God's plan, as seen through the Abrahamic covenant in the book of Genesis and the admonition to fill the whole earth. The people at Babel desired to make a name for themselves so that they would not be scattered over the face of the earth. When God saw their plan, He implemented a solution of His own that would decimate their prideful plan.

> But the LORD came down to see the city and the tower which the sons of men had built. And the LORD said, "Indeed the people are one and they all have one language, and this is what they begin to

do; now nothing that they propose to do will be withheld from them. Come, let Us go down and there confuse their language, that they may not understand one another's speech." (Genesis 11:5–7)

Notice God said, *"Let Us."* In this statement, He emphasized the need to keep people's groups distinct. The trinity—Father, Son, and Holy Spirit—underlined the need for nations to retain uniqueness. This protects humankind from the pride and arrogance of a few who would limit our ability to bring glory to our Creator. People groups must retain their distinctness, language, and customs, so that humanity may be kept from coming under a small group of leaders—or a leader—who could be tainted by arrogance and could fight for greater and greater power and authority.

Genesis 11:8–9 emphasizes this when it says, *"So the Lord scattered them from there over all the earth, and they stopped building the city. That is why it was called Babel—because there the Lord confused the language of the whole world"* (NIV). The true meaning of this passage is lost in modern English translations but found in the ancient language spoken in the days of Noah's early descendants. The Assyrian language was spoken at this time, and the word babel in Assyrian means "gate of God." The Assyrian word "Bab-il" is recorded in the Hebrew text "Babel" and thus into English "Babel."

It never meant nonsensical words; rather, the nonsensical words were the strategy of God used to shut the "gate" to the first attack of a demonic globalist agenda.

The Tower of Babel stands in history as a positive story of the need to decentralize power. This was the first time God biblically established a plan to protect people from consolidated power, allowing a select few to control the masses. The godless agenda to centralize authority, unify language, and merge national heritages into a single entity is a timeless struggle. One world government focusing on man's wisdom is a fight we will have until the end of time.

In Genesis 12, we find the first stages of God's redemptive plan through Abraham. God told him, *"Get out of your country, from your family and from your father's house, to a land that I will show you. I will make you a great nation; I will bless you and make your name great; and you shall be a blessing. I will bless those who bless you, and I will curse him who curses you; and in you all the families of the earth shall be blessed"* (Genesis 12:1–3).

Remember that the call to be gatekeepers comes just after the Tower of Babel. Genesis 9–11 brings the importance of the Abrahamic covenant to light. God is *for* the Abrahamic covenant, His way of protecting and blessing His people, and *against* the anti-Semitic spirit that desires to centralize control and power. We must fight this spirit diligently and oppose the centralization of control and power by evil tyrants. As we consider possessing the gates of the enemy, blessing nations, and impacting generations, the Tower of Babel must be looked upon thoughtfully.

God's call to bless the nations and possess the gates protects them from the enemy's plan of the centralized power of tyrants. This truth goes back to Genesis 1:28, which tells us to *"fill the earth."*

We must never be satisfied with consolidated power and the downplaying of a national heritage. Boundaries are in place for one reason: to protect us. Languages are established to keep us unique. Efforts for any nation to be a global partner must always be pursued cautiously and seen as temporary.

So, should we return to the Tower of Babel? Yes, absolutely. Returning to the Tower of Babel means having an outlook that checks the pride and arrogance of leaders by inviting the trinity to protect us from the plans of a few who would oppose God and His plan for our nation. The promise to possess the gates refers to a city—we must focus on our nation, states, and cities, remembering that, in the Old Testament, groups of people, clans, and cities are comparable to nations.

EIGHTEEN

MODERN-DAY TOWERS OF BABEL

Throughout history, humans have attempted to construct towers of Babel—human-made structures to bring glory to themselves and to keep other people under their control. In earlier eras that were less technologically advanced, conquerors sought to establish their empires using force and power. However, these empires were not as enduring or prosperous as the ideological empires of today. The contemporary ideological structures are founded on philosophical principles or lines of reasoning.

If we are going to be gatekeepers who bless our nation and impact generations worldwide, we must recognize the new empires being constructed. We must be wise and discerning to watch as if protecting ourselves against portals of evil. Only with this perspective can we intercede effectively and hear from God to know how to cooperate with His leading.

TOWER NUMBER ONE: DIALECTICAL MATERIALISM

One of these new empires, which began during the Enlightenment of the 1800s, was spearheaded by Joseph Dietzgen, known as the "philosopher of socialism."

Dietzgen wrote a famous collection of essays that includes a series of six "sermons" entitled "The Religion of Social-Democracy." Many of the disturbing philosophies propounded today came from Dietzgen over one hundred and fifty years ago:

- "In the old religion man served the gospel, in the new religion the gospel is to serve man."
- "The law exists for our sake, to serve us, and to be modified to our needs."
- "The old gospel required of us patience and submissiveness; the new gospel requires of us energy and activity."
- "In the place of grace it puts conscious work."
- "The old bible was named authority and faith; the new has for its title revolutionary science."
- "Work is the name of the new Redeemer."
- "The world is over-populated...."
- "Social-democracy...deeply desires justice for all."
- "the social order of the future make all men equal in rank and value...."
- "Humanity...is the bodily representation...of divine perfection."
- "Civilized...society is the supreme being...."

- "To socialism we build our hope."
- "In the place of religion, social-democracy puts *humanity*...."
- "Its savior can only be found in co-operative, brotherly work: in economic communism."[45]

Dietzgen identified a demonic strategy for powering cultural change. He called it dialectic materialism. Dialectic materialism describes how sinful tension (dialectic) exists naturally (materialism) because of man's fall. An example of this tension would be that which exists between the working class and business owners. The working class may envy the business owners' wealth, which is sometimes fueled by greed. This demonic strategy became Marxist philosophy.

The effects of dialectic materialism are evident everywhere. There are the affluent and the impoverished, the oppressed and their oppressors. Socialism and communist leaders have wielded sin as a lever for transformation. Greed, envy, and power lust are seen as instruments for constructing their Tower of Babel. Examining protest movements over the last century reveals a consistent pattern of categorizing groups in this manner, leading to dire consequences. Recently, this division has prominently featured in movements like Occupy Wall Street, Black Lives Matter, Antifa, and the conflict between Palestine and Hamas with Israel.

> **We must be wise and discerning to watch as if protecting ourselves against portals of evil.**

---

45. Joseph Dietzgen, *Some of the Philosophical Essays on Socialism and Science, Religion, Ethics, Critique-of-Reason and the World-at-Large* (Chicago, IL: Charles H. Kerr & Company, 1906), 91, 94, 97, 100, 106–107, 109.

TOWER NUMBER TWO: CRITICAL RACE THEORY

Critical race theory, or CRT, is a movement that has recently become a cultural flashpoint. CRT was birthed from previous movements, critical legal studies and feminism, and from "certain European philosophers and theorists, such as Antonio Gramsci, Michel Foucault, and Jacques Derrida."[46]

CRT also owes some of its history to Marxist tenets and "examines the very foundations of the liberal order, including equality theory, legal reasoning, Enlightenment rationalism, and neutral principles of constitutional law."[47] This movement that was first seen in legal academia has permeated some businesses, schools, government agencies, and churches.

One of the most vocal opponents of CRT is Christopher Rufo, who writes, "In simple terms, critical race theory reformulates the old Marxist dichotomy of oppressor and oppressed, replacing the class categories of bourgeoisie and proletariat with the identity categories of White and Black. But the basic conclusion is the same: to liberate man, society must be fundamentally transformed through moral, economic, and political revolution."[48]

As we established in chapter 6, man is inherently flawed. The Marxist ideals repackaged with new labels are the same ineffective strategy attempting to make the nature of imperfect man. The following strategy capitalizes on the imperfection of man. "Christians don't need CRT to live biblically regarding race because a kingdom-shaped worldview already supports most of what CRT seeks to rectify. Genuine CRT concepts aren't antithetical to a Christian worldview."[49]

---

46. Richard Delgado and Jean Stefancic, *Critical Race Theory: An Introduction*, Fourth Edition (New York: New York University Press, 2023), 4
47. Delgado and Stefancic, *Critical Race Theory*, 3.
48. Christopher F. Rufo, "Critical Race Theory Briefing Book," accessed January 29, 2025, https://christopherrufo.com/p/crt-briefing-book.
49. Ed Uszynski, *Untangling Critical Race Theory: What Christians Need to Know and Why It Matters* (Lisle, IL: IVP, 2024), 81.

TOWER NUMBER THREE: THE CLOWARD-PIVEN STRATEGY

The Cloward-Piven Strategy, developed by Richard Cloward and Frances Fox Piven, is another road map to control a nation. This strategy, outlined in 1966, aimed to mobilize political change by overloading the welfare system through increasing welfare claims. Cloward and Fox Piven sought "to wipe out poverty by establishing a guaranteed annual income"[50] through their strategy. This will cause more discontent, and it will be easier to tax (take from) the rich with the support of the poor.

The presentation of the strategy makes it clear that the changes in the United States are neither random nor merely a cultural evolution over time. These adjustments are intentional and have been achieved through years of dedicated effort.

TOWER NUMBER FOUR: IDEOLOGICAL SUBVERSION

Yuri Bezmenov, a former KGB agent who defected to the West, revealed a tactic employed by the Soviet Union and other Communist nations to shape and mold society through a cyclical four-step process similar to societal brainwashing.

STEP 1: DEMORALIZATION

Demoralization, a process that can take fifteen to twenty years, destroys faith in the government and society. Guilt is not only an immensely effective tool for changing behavior and mindsets but also for promoting a desire for more government. Three key beliefs are cultivated: society is broken, systems are failing, and patriotism is evil. Demoralization removes the ability to process information correctly and skews reality.

---

50. Frances Fox Piven and Richard Cloward, "The Weight of the Poor: A Strategy to End Poverty," *The Nation*, March 8, 2010, https://www.thenation.com/article/archive/weight-poor-strategy-end-poverty/.

STEP 2: DESTABILIZATION

After demoralization, the next step is destabilizing the nation's foundations. Attacks on the economy, political systems, national culture, and essential institutions begin and become more successful with the belief that the nation's systems are not worth preserving or defending. The goal is to foster criticism of the foundational institutions of a nation so that traditional authority will not be trusted. As a result, what is harmful is called good, and people who disagree are now enemies.

STEP 3: CRISIS

At the crisis stage, the altered values may lay an axe to the root of the current systems. Upheaval presents opportunities for change. Once a society is destabilized, it quickly collapses into chaos and crisis. At this point, citizens *want* the government to provide stability.

STEP 4: NORMALIZATION

When the government and societal structures have changed, citizens are told it is "the way it has to be." Ironically, what is not normal at all is described as normal. Messaging reorients citizens to the new way and defuses resistance.

This four-stage process is cyclical and will repeat itself. I have seen this process at work in America over the last fifty years or more. We also see the cyclical aspects of current societal divisions and political polarization.

The ideological towers of Babel have other names, such as social democracy, socialism, communism, progressivism, and so on. However, it is all the same: a demonic strategy that utilizes sinful desires to accomplish cultural change. This philosophy's advent was initially fueled by books distributed in universities worldwide. Then, as it took a foothold in countries, it became a part of government education.

TOWER NUMBER FIVE: GLOBALISM

Today, the ease of travel and the exponential effect of technology require intercession with divine effectiveness because the next phase is globalism. Organizations such as the World Economic Forum, the United Nations, and the World Health Organization connect nations to yield national sovereignty in favor of global efforts and governance. This trend has spiritual roots in the New Age movement, which arose from the Theosophical Society.

Founded in 1875 by Helena Blavatsky and Henry Olcott, around the time Dietzgen wrote his pre-Marxist sermons, the Theosophical Society is a global occult movement focused on universal brotherhood; the comparative study of religion, philosophy, and science; and investigating the unexplained laws of nature.[51] The original emblem and logo say, "There is no religion higher than truth."[52] It features a menagerie of symbols, including a swastika, the ankh, the star of David, and the Om symbol, among others. Blavatsky and Olcott led the early theosophical movement into worldwide popularity. Blavatsky was heralded as the "greatest Occultist of the West" and an "outstanding messenger who presented the Ancient Wisdom for the modern age."[53]

This occult movement views the United Nations as a key organization for achieving their religious goals. "Theosophists believe that the nations of the world constitute a single humanity—a single human community. The United Nations is but the physical demonstration

---

51. "What do Theosophists Believe," The Theosophical Society, accessed January 28, 2025, https://www.theosophical.org/about/theosophy.
52. "Theosophy and Science," The Theosophical Society, accessed January 28, 2025, https://www.theosophical.org/component/content/article/theosophy-and-science?catid=25&Itemid=1107.
53. "Helena Petrovna Blavatsky," TS Adyar, accessed February 18, 2025, https://www.ts-adyar.org/helena-petrovna-blavatsky-1831-1891.

of our concept of Universal Brotherhood," stated theosophist Diana Gracey Winslow.⁵⁴

Theosophical International President N. Sri Ram elaborated on this in the May 1957 edition of *On the Watch Tower*: "The United Nations is an organisation which is obviously meant to develop into a bone-frame for a new body of humanity. The whole of humanity has to be organized in such a way so that it can function as one body, though divided into different States, and this new body has to be upheld by a structure which will express its common will and purpose."⁵⁵

Alice Bailey and her Master Masonic husband, Foster Bailey, were heavily involved in the Theosophical Society and birthed the modern New Age movement. From the beginning, Bailey saw the importance of the UN in achieving her religious vision. "Within the United Nations is the germ and the seed of a great international and meditating, reflective group—a group of thinking and informed men and women in whose hands lies the destiny of humanity. This is largely under the control of many fourth ray disciples...."⁵⁶

Can you see the success of Bailey's efforts in the United States? It is interesting to note that the Baileys founded Lucifer Publishing Company, now called Lucis Trust—a UN-recognized NGO that holds spirituality seminars, services, and training within the UN.

The call to bless the nations and impact generations has never been as important or challenging as it is today. Being gatekeepers in the days of physical gates was much easier to accomplish. Now, ideological seats of authority can be influenced by a keystroke. The need for wise,

---

54. Diana Gracey Winslow, "A Theosophist Looks at the United Nations Organization," *The Theosophist*, November 1953, https://international.theoservice.org/news/TS%20and%20UN.pdf.
55. N. Sri Ram, "Selections from the Theosophist," *On the Watch Tower* (Theosophical Publishing House, 1966).
56. Alice A. Bailey, *Discipleship in the New Age, Volume II* (Lucis Trust, 1994), https://www.lucistrust.org/online_books/discipleship_in_the_new_age_vol_ii_obooks/section_two_teachings_on_meditation_part5.

discerning intercession is critical and must be considered with fresh eyes. I am reminded of 2 Corinthians 10:4–5: *"The weapons we fight with are not the weapons of this world. On the contrary, they have divine power to demolish strongholds. We demolish arguments and every pretension that sets itself up against the knowledge of God"* (NIV).

SECTION 4:

WHERE ARE WE HEADING?

NINETEEN

GLOBAL CRESCENDO OF FREEDOM

America was among the first entities to be established as a free nation where the people governed themselves. It was founded by a group of people who believed they could create a government based on biblical principles. It was radical and revolutionary, yet they built a nation that grew to become a global gatekeeper.

The fact that so many elections occur worldwide demonstrates the radical and far-reaching impact that America has had and continues to have on the entire world. Dictators now feel that they have to hold elections. Why? The American experiment elevated and celebrated freedom, awakening people's thirst for it worldwide.

When I first received the revelation that whoever controls the gates of a city controls that city, I was astounded. I had been in the governmental intercession sector for over fifteen years and had never heard anyone teach on this subject. Controlling the gates is possessing the gates of the enemy, as described in the book of Genesis:

> By Myself I have sworn, says the LORD, because you have done this thing, and have not withheld your son, your only son—blessing I will bless you, and multiplying I will multiply your descendants as the stars of the heaven and as the sand which is on the seashore; and your descendants shall possess the gate of their enemies.
> (Genesis 22:16–17)

As we see from Scripture, part of our Abrahamic covenant is to possess the gates of the enemy. We see this covenantal promise confirmed in Genesis 24:60: "And they blessed Rebekah and said to her: 'Our sister, may you become the mother of thousands of ten thousands; and may your descendants possess the gates of those who hate them.'"

Intercession reveals direction. Intercession dispatches discernment and releases the destiny of individuals and nations. Intercession brings to completion the promises made.

Let's journey now to the global crescendo of freedom. As the body of Christ, it is time we gain a different outlook on culture and our involvement in governmental affairs. We must give the Holy Spirit permission to adjust our thinking to the revelation of how we begin to actively possess the gates of the enemy.

The year 2024 was a year like no other year in human history. It was a year of a historical culmination, a crescendo of global freedom, especially concerning elections. Sixty-six countries had scheduled elections in 2024. At no other time in humanity's history have more elections been planned in one year. Are we possessing the gates of our enemies with the values of freedom?

Moving forward, we must understand the importance of elections and consider what God is doing around the globe in the light of His calling for all of us to possess the gates of the enemy. Less than three hundred years ago, not a single country in the world offered citizens the opportunity to participate in the election of those who would have authority over them. I don't think many people realize this vital fact.

Three hundred years ago, there were no free elections in any nation. The Declaration of Independence and the Constitution of the United States initially set free elections in motion and established a democratic process to determine the country's leaders.

Slowly, over time, the idea of the freedoms our founding fathers championed crept across the globe. The founding fathers believed God alone gave us our rights. That belief impacted the way our nation elects officials and the way it upholds freedom. The desire for freedom is infectious and has grown worldwide.

The very fact that it is God who gave us our rights impacted the way our nation chooses its leaders. Ever so slowly, country after country began to adopt this idea of free elections. It was based on the freedoms on display in the United States.

By the year 1900, 25 percent of the global population could participate in some way of selecting their leaders. A mere one hundred years later, the percentage grew to 50 percent of the worldwide population participating in free elections. Over the last twenty years, this statistic has grown to the point where two-thirds, or six billion of the eight billion people on the earth, can participate in elections. Three hundred short years ago, there were zero. Now, we are at two-thirds of the world's population. This movement of participatory elections is evidence of possessing the gates—statistical, demonstrable evidence. We can see that this is one way God's people can influence the seat of authority and possess the enemy's gates.

> *Intercession reveals direction. Intercession dispatches discernment and releases the destiny of individuals and nations. Intercession brings to completion the promises made.*

Free elections have indeed been infectious and have spread around the world. You're seeing the biblical covenant in action. The biblical mandate is in real-time, statistically. We are seeing a crescendo of the Abrahamic covenant: to possess gates and to be a blessing to the nations.

Looking back in history, a founding group of leaders established a biblical form of government. In 1776, those ideas swept the globe and now bless nations worldwide. Blessing other nations is another part of our Abrahamic covenant. It started with the United States of America and the longest-lasting Constitution in the history of humankind. I'm thankful we get to live in a day when we see this happening.

TWENTY

GOD'S DESIGN FOR GOVERNMENT

I am thankful we live in a nation established in God. Certain things will prove vital if we are to continue to see the United States of America succeed and flourish. One of those things is a good government. Good government is essential for nations to thrive. When nations thrive, their people find fulfillment. Secular research confirms this truth established in the Word of God.

GOOD GOVERNMENT IS ESSENTIAL FOR NATIONS TO THRIVE

Consolidated findings from the International Monetary Fund, the World Bank, and Statista indicate nations thrive when their governments focus on reducing corruption, emphasizing the rule of law, and ensuring a trustworthy electoral process. Such governments produce the most satisfied and economically productive inhabitants, fostering a sense of security and optimism. Such a government has leaders with integrity who consistently apply the rule of law and are governed by the will of their people.

Government is a divine creation. A template for effective government is found in Exodus 18:21–26:

> *"Moreover you shall select from all the people able men, such as fear God, men of truth, hating covetousness; and place such over them to be rulers of thousands, rulers of hundreds, rulers of fifties, and rulers of tens. And let them judge the people at all times. Then it will be that every great matter they shall bring to you, but every small matter they themselves shall judge. So it will be easier for you, for they will bear the burden with you. If you do this thing, and God so commands you, then you will be able to endure, and all this people will also go to their place in peace." So Moses heeded the voice of his father-in-law and did all that he had said. And Moses chose able men out of all Israel and made them heads over the people: rulers of thousands, rulers of hundreds, rulers of fifties, and rulers of tens. So they judged the people at all times; the hard cases they brought to Moses, but they judged every small case themselves.*

This genesis of global freedoms is found in the Old Testament. The first representative republic is found in the Old Testament. The first representative republic since Old Testament times that still operates today is the United States.

RELIGIOUS FREEDOM IS VITAL FOR CHURCHES TO THRIVE

Regarding people's day-to-day lives, what is the most essential element for their finding fulfillment? For this answer, we turn to a global Pew Research Center study of over twenty-five nations that indicates that "actively religious people are more likely than their less-religious peers to describe themselves as "very happy" in about half of the countries surveyed."[57] In twenty-five countries, secular researchers discovered that people find the most fulfillment when they are part of a faith community.[58] This goes back to God's original design and what Jesus came to establish—the church. In doing so, He declared that the gates of hell shall not prevail against His church. (See Matthew 16:18.)

So, as we consider praying for increasing global freedoms, including good government and religious liberty, which are essential for societal well-being, let's examine one final point.

HEALTHY FAMILIES ARE VITAL FOR OUR CITY, STATE, AND NATION TO THRIVE

What is it that produces the most well-adjusted and economically successful people? The answer to this can be found in numerous studies, including the American Enterprise Institute study, which concluded that children who grow up in two-parent homes are more behaviorally adjusted and have more economic success than those raised in single-parent homes.[59]

Many children grow up in one-parent households, but does that mean they cannot thrive? Certainly not. Yet, the truth remains that children have a better chance of thriving if raised in a two-parent home, according to God's original design. Children who grow up in a one-parent home are not doomed, but nations should *promote* a two-parent household with a mother and father present. Additionally, economic studies have determined that the financial stability of same-sex couples

---

57. Joey Marshall, "Are Religious People Happier, Healthier? Our New Global Study Explores This Question," *Pew Research Center*, January 31, 2019, https://www.pewresearch.org/short-reads/2019/01/31/are-religious-people-happier-healthier-our-new-global-study-explores-this-question/.
58. "Religion's Relationship to Happiness, Civic Engagement and Health Around the World," *Pew Research Center*, January 31, 2019, https://www.pewresearch.org/religion/2019/01/31/religions-relationship-to-happiness-civic-engagement-and-health-around-the-world/.
59. Brad Wilcox and David Bass, "Growing Up in Intact Families Matters More Than Ever," *The American Enterprise Institute*, October 2, 2023, https://www.aei.org/articles/growing-up-in-intact-families-matters-more-than-ever/.

raising children significantly lags behind the economic success of families that include a mom and a dad.[60]

As we can see, the vital components of possessing the gates of the enemy, blessing nations, and impacting generations include good government, thriving faith communities, and healthy two-parent families. This is how God designed it to be. May we return to His original plan, inspired and motivated to make a positive change.

God created these three institutions to care for us: the government cares for us civilly, the church cares for us spiritually, and family cares for us individually.

Freedom. Faith. Family. These three words roll off our tongues and are evidence of a truth written upon our hearts.

Each institution has its proper role and scope of jurisdiction. If the church takes on too much of the role of the family, it becomes a cult. If the government takes on the church's role, it transforms into a morally vacant welfare state. If the government takes too much of the role of the family, it becomes socialism. The constant spiritual battle is around the points of intersection.

> *God created these three institutions to care for us: the government cares for us civilly, the church cares for us spiritually, and family cares for us individually.*

In the beginning, God made a covenant promise to Abraham that his descendants—and that includes us—would possess the gates of their enemies. This covenant has not been completely fulfilled; it is

---

60. M. V. Lee Badgett, Laura E. Durso, Alyssa Schneebaum, "New Patterns of Poverty in the Lesbian, Gay, and Bisexual Community," *UCLA School of Law The Williams Institute*, June 2013, https://williamsinstitute.law.ucla.edu/publications/lgb-patterns-of-poverty/.

still being fulfilled today. Blessing nations and impacting generations involves restoring God's original purpose and destiny for governments without allowing them to overshadow the family or restrict our religious freedoms.

TWENTY-ONE

HAVING HOPE IN THE END TIMES

Some say, "Jesus is coming back, so why should I care about my nation?" Christians in every generation have believed that Jesus would come back in their lifetime. Every generation is entrusted with urgently spreading the news of Christ's kingdom.

Jesus said, in Matthew 24:12–13, *"And because lawlessness will abound, the love of many will grow cold. But he who endures to the end shall be saved."* Do we see a time of increased wickedness? Do we see some who have grown cold? Yes, we do. However, those who stand firm to the end will be saved. What's the timetable that Jesus lays out? Jesus continued, *"And this gospel of the kingdom will be preached in all the world as a witness to all the nations, **and then** the end will come"* (Matthew 24:14).

What gospel was Jesus talking about? He didn't say salvation. No, it's broader than that. It's the kingdom. That's an essential distinction in this passage. In this time, Jesus was speaking of the gospel of the kingdom that would be preached to the whole world. God's values and kingdom ways would be preached to *all the nations*.

Jesus told the disciples that their generation would not pass until the unfolding of the second coming. (See Matthew 24:34.) This was in the hearts of His disciples. The second coming was imminent. It could even have been in their lifetime. At least, that's what they thought. What would have happened if they had stopped sharing the gospel because they thought Jesus would come back? What about the next generation? What about our generation? We cannot let it stop with us. When Jesus said His second coming would occur in their lifetime, He talked about the unfolding of His second coming through His church. He was talking about preaching the gospel of His kingdom throughout the globe.

> *God's values and kingdom ways would be preached to all the nations.*

Some Christians look at Matthew 24:12 and suggest that since the rise of evil (lawlessness) will be unstoppable, it is pointless to try to influence the government. However, that is not what Jesus said. He said evil would increase, and the gospel of the kingdom will be preached. Then He would come again. Between the increase of evil and His physical second coming, the gospel will be preached to all the nations. Evil will increase, and the gospel will spread. Then He will return. That's the pattern. It is not the time to give up; just the opposite. It's time for the good news of this kingdom to go to all nations: salvation and freedom through Christ. Knowing this truth, the rise of evil should encourage us. Why? Because it is in this environment where the goodness of God becomes clear, and people respond to Him in ways that we've never seen before.

When the rise of evil is evident (and it is), the gospel of the kingdom will go forth (and it must). The contrast between darkness and light highlights the need for the moral absolutes of the timeless principles found in the Bible. We are seeing today what Jesus described. Evil is increasing, and the kingdom of God is going forth.

In the past few years, Isaiah 60:1–3 has been highlighted to me by the Lord and has been shared by others as a prophetic passage speaking of the end times.

> *Arise, shine; for your light has come! And the glory of the LORD is risen upon you. For behold, the darkness shall cover the earth, and deep darkness the people; but the LORD will arise over you, and His glory will be seen upon you.* (Isaiah 60:1–3)

These words, written centuries ago, look forward to the time when God's glory will come to the earth in one final crescendo. His glory will outmatch the increase of evil. These are the days we live in, days of unspeakable evil, and yet days where the glory of God will come upon us like never before. I believe we are in a time of the greatest activity of God through the church—more than any other time in history. I count it a privilege to be alive today. Jesus isn't caught off guard by what He is seeing. He will use everything happening in the world, as well as you and me, to possess the enemy's gates. We are privileged to be a part of the fulfillment of the Abrahamic covenant.

There are some well-known verses in the book of Isaiah that remind us ultimately whose responsibility it is to fight these battles:

> *For unto us a Child is born, unto us a Son is given; and the government will be upon His shoulder. And His name will be called Wonderful, Counselor, Mighty God, Everlasting Father, Prince of Peace. Of the increase of His government and peace there will be no end, upon the throne of David and over His kingdom, to order it*

and establish it with judgment and justice from that time forward, even forever. The zeal of the LORD of hosts will perform this.

(Isaiah 9:6–7)

These verses, most famous for being read during the Christmas season, have always intrigued me. Of course, we understand that God gave us His Son in the form of a child. But what about this: the government will be on His shoulders, and His government and peace will keep increasing? How could this be? Is this true? Is this happening today?

It seems we are watching the powers of darkness increase daily. Through prayer and intercession, we have battled spiritual wickedness for our great nation—a nation that has received countless prophetic words. Yet its government seems more corrupt than ever. Does Jesus really know what He is doing?!

I want to suggest to you that when we take a long-term, historical view of Jesus's government, we can only conclude that it has increased and that His rule will never end.

The first increase of Jesus's government is the historical growth of His rule over personal lives. The book of Acts tells us that the very first group of believers that placed themselves under Jesus's rule, under His government, numbered about one hundred and twenty. This small band of believers hid from the public eye until the Holy Spirit fell upon them at Pentecost. That day, Peter preached, and the number of people under Jesus's government grew to 3,000. Signs, wonders, and persecution followed; Saul was converted, and the gospel spread from Jerusalem to Judea to all parts of the world.

From the early days of the New Testament, more hearts have embraced the lordship of Jesus over their lives, decade after decade, century after century. There were maybe 200,000 by the year 200 AD; by the end of the fifth century, there were ten million hearts. In the early 1900s, Pew Research estimated that the global population of followers of Christ was 600 million, and now, after just 100 more years, that number has grown to about 2.4 billion—one-third of the global population practices Christianity.

There is no doubt the increase of Christ's government over the lives of individuals is never-ending and always on the rise.[61]

The second clear indication of His government's expansion lies in the civil arena. The Scriptures' model for civil government is unique: God grants us personal rights and makes laws. "This truth about the nature of personal rights, personal freedoms, and law has been at odds with dictators, kings, and autocrats throughout history. And yet, over the centuries, people yearned and fought for the freedom that God hardwired in us. At the beginning of the second millennium, the idea that we all have rights began to take hold through documents like the Magna Carta, philosophers such as Augustine, and legal scholars."[62] All of this swirling of ideas fueled the God-given desire of people to be free—to worship the God they choose and speak their minds.

Following the First Great Awakening in the 1700s, when 50,000 Americans embraced Jesus's governance, a divinely inspired vision of government took shape. A small group of people were inspired by God to establish a nation, recognizing that our Creator has endowed all of us with equal rights, including life, liberty, and the pursuit of happiness. The framers of the American Constitution understood that the strongest government derives its power solely from the free consent of the governed.

For the first time *in world history*, a government acknowledged that our rights come from God and that the only moral government is one led by elected, willing, and free citizens.

---

61. David Kubal, "June 9, 2023, The Increase of His Government," *Give Him 15*, June 9, 2023, https://www.givehim15.com/post/june-9-2023.
62. Kubal, "June 9, 2023."

From America's inception, this nation has illustrated how the yearning for freedom shapes governance worldwide. In the past 300 years, the percentage of people with the freedom and privilege to elect their leaders has gone from 0 percent to 85 percent.[63]

"Our Founding Fathers put in place a nation whose freedoms were so compelling that the entire world was changed. There are certainly variations of free elections, but the point remains":[64] *"the increase of His government"* (Isaiah 9:7) is not ending; it is increasing.

There is undeniable and widely accepted evidence that Jesus's influence has expanded over time. Initially, a small group of frightened disciples has grown to include 2.4 billion people, representing one-third of today's global population. There were once no civil governments reflecting the God-given aspiration for personal freedom, but now, over 80 percent of global governments strive to project at least the appearance of freedom. I love how the *New International Version* translates this verse: *"Of the greatness of his government and peace there will be no end"* (Isaiah 9:7 NIV).

At the end of Isaiah 9:7, Isaiah prophesied, *"The zeal of the LORD Almighty will accomplish this"* (NIV). The term "zeal," referred to as *qinah* in Hebrew, is fascinating. In Hebrew, zeal appears only a few times. Each instance of the phrase *"the zeal of the LORD"* in the Bible guarantees that the promise will be fulfilled without fail. Additionally, we often encounter phrases like *"great fury"* (see Daniel 11:44) and *"consuming fire"* (see Psalm 18:8 NIV).

What is the bottom line of this passage? In pursuing God's will for our nation, we have His zeal to support and guide us. For our nation to receive God's blessings, followers of Jesus Christ must take a stand today, proclaim His governance, seek the Prince of Peace, and strive

---

63. "Countries That are Democracies and Autocracies, World," Our World in Data, accessed February 18, 2025, https://ourworldindata.org/grapher/countries-democracies-autocracies-row.
64. Kubal, "June 9, 2023."

for His justice and righteousness, both personally and collectively, as a nation. My friend, that is good news!

There is no better way to close than with prayer:

Lord, You have inscribed the principles of good governance in our hearts. You have instilled a longing for freedom within all of creation. As we observe the forces of darkness striving to undermine our religious freedoms and freedom of speech, we pray that You would empower Your church in this time. Lord, help Your body understand that You have a vision for government, You desire a just government, and Your government is founded on genuine justice and righteousness.

Thank You for instilling in us an unquenchable thirst for freedom. Thank You for guiding us as we reflect on the ages and witness Your powerful hand at work as Your government expands. Thank You that we are here for such a time as this. Thank You for allowing us to see the fulfillment of the Abrahamic covenant, in Jesus's name.

We declare from Your Word that the government's duty lies with our Lord Jesus Christ, who is the Wonderful Counselor, the Mighty God, the Everlasting Father, and the Prince of Peace. His reign will never cease to expand. We proclaim that the zeal of the Lord Almighty will bring this to fruition. We will witness the realization of the Abrahamic covenant through Jesus's name. Amen.

ABOUT THE AUTHOR

David Kubal is CEO/President of Intercessors for America, a massive grassroots organization uniting millions of citizens to pray and take action on the issues confronting America. Equipping Christians to engage and speak truth into the important cultural debates of our day, Kubal is a nationally recognized faith leader and serves as a faith advisor on the National Faith Advisory Board that advises the highest leaders in America. He also serves on the National Day of Prayer Task Force, National Prayer Committee Board, and International Christian Jewish Embassy, and he is an advisor to Christians Engaged.

Kubal brings over thirty-five years of national ministry experience, is seminary trained and ordained in the Evangelical Presbyterian Church, and is a former vice president of the Fellowship of Christian Athletes.

Kubal has appeared on *Real America's Voice*, *Newsmax*, *Victory News*, *Water Cooler with David Brody*, *FlashPoint*, NTD Television, CBN, and other media outlets. He has authored *We Declare: 31 Days of Intercession for America*; *Inspired Prayers: Praying the Scripture Promises That Motivated Our Founding Fathers*; *Inspired People: Ten People God Inspired Who Changed Our Nation*; and *Fasting: Accelerating God's*

Activity in Your Life and the Life of Our Nation, which is published in the *Washington Times, Newsmax, Fox News, The Stream,* and other print and online publications. David also co-authored *Inspired Stories 50 Years of Answered Prayer.* Kubal has also been a featured speaker at national conferences and events, from the Western Conservative Summit to NFL chapels. Kubal and his family reside in the greater Washington, DC, area.

News. Prayer. Action.

Want to impact *generations*?

Join a community of ordinary people fulfilling their extraordinary destiny by praying for the nations.

Learn what it means to live out the Abrahamic covenant daily.

You can join IFA by going to **ifapray.org/impact**, or by scanning the QR code below:

We can't wait to pray with you!

Welcome to Our House!

We Have a Special Gift for You

It is our privilege and pleasure to share in your love of Christian books. We are committed to bringing you authors and books that feed, challenge, and enrich your faith.

To show our appreciation, we invite you to sign up to receive a specially selected **Reader Appreciation Gift**, with our compliments. Just go to the Web address at the bottom of this page.

God bless you as you seek a deeper walk with Him!

WE HAVE A GIFT FOR YOU. VISIT:

whpub.me/nonfictionthx

Whitaker House